"In the midst of a season filled with so m[...]
has seemed like an impossible ask. And yet, as I read through
these pages, I found my heart encouraged and convicted by
Allison's gentle, biblical, and real-life counsel—showing us that
gratitude isn't just about "thinking positive" but that it's a posture
of the heart that impacts every facet of the Christian life."

SARAH WALTON, *Coauthor, Hope When It Hurts, Together through the Storms, and He Gives More Grace*

"In her new book, *Grateful: 30 Days of Growing in Thankfulness,*
my friend and the author Allison Brost dives into the complexities
of acknowledging the challenging, discouraging, and messy
moments in life, all while still positioning ourselves before the
Lord in gratitude and thanksgiving for all that he has done and
all he will still do, as we surrender our lives to his will and his
way. Through her own grief and personal trials, Allison has built
her life on the immovable truth of God's goodness. Her continual
desire to posture herself before God with a grateful heart will be
inspiring to all her readers."

TABITHA YATES, *Author, Jesus and Therapy; Writer at The Redeemed Mama*

"The pain and suffering that give Allison Brost every reason to
grumble are what make her the perfect voice to exhort readers
to be grateful. At no point will they think, "Easy for her to say,"
because none of this is. Allison has tilled and toiled to cultivate
gratitude in her own life and offers this book as a gardening
guide to help others grow in gratefulness as well. Her action
steps at the end of each devotion artfully allow for immediate
application without encouraging self-reliance. As she writes, "It
takes intentionality to grow gratefully," and, with the help of the
Master Gardener, *Grateful* is precisely the tool you need to do it."

ABBEY WEDGEWORTH, *Author, Held and the Training Young Hearts series*

"In *Grateful,* Allison leads us to cultivate a thankful heart even in this imperfect life. She teaches us to practice gratitude every day, no matter what it brings. She doesn't shy away from the hard stuff of this life but instead points us to Scripture and teaches us to seek things to be grateful for right in the midst of it."

KELSEY SCISM, *Author, One Year with Jesus: A Weekly Devotional Journal for Middle School Girls*

"Allison Brost doesn't claim to have perfected what it means to live a life of gratitude; but with refreshing authenticity and a humble posture, she uses God's word to challenge readers to pause, reflect, and take actionable steps to begin growing in thankfulness."

JESSIKA SANDERS, *Coauthor, In His Hands; Executive Director, Praying Through Ministries*

"I found that these short and simple reflections really resonated with me and stirred my heart to thank God. These chapters revealed how much more God has been doing than I was aware of! A precious little book that will do your heart good."

LINDA ALLCOCK, *Author, Deeper Still*

"In *Grateful,* Allison opens our eyes to the goodness of God despite our circumstances. Through relatable stories and practical guidance, Allison takes her readers lovingly by the heart and leads them to experience true, lasting gratitude in the Lord."

AMBER PALMER, *Writer at My Jars of Clay*

Grateful

30 DAYS OF GROWING IN THANKFULNESS

Grateful
30 DAYS OF GROWING IN THANKFULNESS

ALLISON BROST

Grateful
30 Days of Growing in Thankfulness

© Allison Brost, 2025

Published by:
The Good Book Company

thegoodbook.com | thegoodbook.co.uk
thegoodbook.com.au | thegoodbook.co.nz | thegoodbook.co.in

Cover design by Jennifer Phelps | Design and art direction by André Parker

ISBN: 9781802541311 | JOB-007973 | Printed in India

To my children, for whom I'm so immensely thankful.
I pray I can leave an example, albeit imperfectly,
of living gratefully.

Contents

Tending the Soil

**CULTIVATING THE GOOD GROUND
OF GRATEFULNESS**

1

God, I Don't
Feel Grateful

*"But I have trusted in your steadfast love;
my heart shall rejoice in your salvation."*

PSALM 13:5

First, I'll admit—writing about gratefulness is intimidating. It's almost like attempting to unlock the secrets behind a successful marriage or sharing the formula to stress-free parenting. I start by wondering whether it's even humanly possible. And then the moment I begin to feel as though I have a thing or two about marriage or parenting figured out, my children or spouse (or just as easily myself!) demonstrate how frail and flawed we humans really are. It's humbling, to say the least.

As I was commiserating with a friend about this, she gently reminded me that maybe this was exactly the attitude I *should* have when writing about this. If I thought I had it all figured out, would that really be glorifying God?

And so it's from this place that I write to you. As a fellow friend who's down in the trenches—fighting the five o'clock frustration when dinner needs to be on the table again and my well-intentioned plans are still a solid block of ice in the back of the freezer, slipping into impatience more easily than calm, and routinely giving into grumbling over glorifying.

The truth is, I don't always feel grateful. And if that's you too, well, I want you to know you're welcome here. I don't know your story, but if you've walked around this broken-down world any length of time, I'm guessing you've experienced your own share of heartaches: strained relationships, tense family dynamics, tight finances… The list could go on and on. Sometimes the things we face in life can make it feel a whole lot easier to give up than give thanks.

Over these chapters, we're going to discover some of the ways we can grow gratefully, uncovering what Scripture says about the power of our thoughts, the importance of focusing on what is true and lovely, and the unshakable truths that point us toward praise for our Creator.

But before we get there, I think it's important that we start here—with honesty. One of the reasons why the Psalms are so special to me is because of the way in which they show the psalmists' humanity. Psalm 13 begins with such a spirit of vulnerability as the writer, David, cries out to God, "How long, O LORD? Will you forget me forever?" Then he goes on in verse 3, "Consider and answer me, O LORD my God; light up my eyes, lest I sleep the sleep of death."

This doesn't sound much like a recipe for thankfulness, does it? But stick with me here for a moment as we pick up in verses 5-6: "But I have trusted in your steadfast love; my heart shall rejoice in your salvation. I will sing to the LORD, because he has dealt bountifully with me." Hear the turnaround David goes through during this passage. Can you sense the profound change from a spirit of discouragement and disappointment to one of trust and, yes, even joy? What is it that causes this seismic shift?

It's simply this: *he brought his thoughts and feelings to God.*

If you're going through something heavy and the last thing you feel is grateful or if you just sense a spiritual dullness about your days, this is where I want to encourage you to start. Begin by telling God exactly how you're feeling. Share with him the deepest worries and weariness of your heart. Lay down your hardest questions and heaviest concerns at his feet. God can handle it *all*.

Being grateful doesn't mean being dishonest about how we feel or hiding what we're going through—it starts with wholeheartedly surrendering it all to him.

Friend, I believe the hard or unexciting parts of your story don't need to lead to a lackluster faith or a downward spiral into discouragement. Perhaps they will actually prove to be the starting point for something so much better—the birthplace of a life that God is growing beautifully grateful.

Cultivate

Come before God with unfiltered honesty; tell him exactly where and how you are struggling to feel thankful. Invite God into these spaces as we begin this 30-day journey. Ask him to breathe new life into what's been broken or dulled and thank him for his promise of renewal.

2

The Choice

"Oh give thanks to the LORD, for he is good;
for his steadfast love endures forever!"

1 CHRONICLES 16:34

It was our church's Thanksgiving Day dinner and the entire sanctuary was brimming—row after row of tables filled with guests, volunteers serving platefuls of food, and a sectioned-off area full of toys for antsy little ones.

Just a few weeks prior, one of the pastors approached my husband to ask whether we might speak at the event. When my husband told me, I gulped. And then I quickly began contemplating all the ways I could tell them no without sounding rude. They wanted *us* to speak?

As I debated over what we could even say, I found myself bogged down with a list of hard realities that felt challenging to sum up and equally difficult to share with a sense of hope. What on earth did we know about gratitude? But slowly God began to meet my misgivings with these words from 1 Thessalonians 5:18: "In everything give thanks" (NKJV).

The words gave me pause. Could that verse really mean

what I thought it said? In the middle of disappointments and everyday inconveniences and circumstances that seemed downright wrong… to give thanks? Not just in the good times or the moments that made sense but in *everything*?

I'd heard this verse many times growing up, but it was one I'd always encountered with a heavy dose of hesitation. I mean, how could I live this way in any practical sense? And how on earth could these words be an encouragement rather than a reminder of all the ways in which I missed the mark?

But in the weeks leading up to that Thanksgiving meal, God began challenging me with this reminder—giving thanks isn't about my *feelings;* it's about *faith.* 1 Chronicles 16:34 is such a powerful reminder of this truth. It says, "Oh give thanks to the LORD, for he is good; for his steadfast love endures forever!"

In the midst of minor irritations and mundane frustrations—*he is good.* In personal disappointments and general discouragements—*his steadfast love endures forever.* Whatever we may be facing, the foundation of gratitude remains firm on these unchangeable truths: *God is good and his steadfast love endures forever.*

This is where I've oftentimes become confused; I've tended to believe that unless I'm *feeling* grateful, I can't *give* thanks— that unless my mind is swarming with happy thoughts and I cease to struggle with grumbling, I'm simply failing at growing in gratitude. But notice here what 1 Thessalonians 5:18 doesn't say. It never tells us that we always have to *feel* thankful. It doesn't tell us to write down ten things we're grateful for each day or remind us to count our blessings more than our burdens, although these can both be beneficial habits. Instead, we're simply commanded to *give thanks.*

You see, God knows that giving thanks may not always fit with how we feel in the moment. At times, it might even feel fake or inconsistent with what we're walking through.

However, all that giving thanks requires is simply *obedience.*

Maybe this does mean taking time to create a list and actively acknowledging things you're thankful for each day. Perhaps it means being aware of critical thoughts and consciously combating complaints with words of gratitude. Or maybe it simply means giving thanks for each small thing as you go about your day. Let God lead you in his grace.

More than an emotion, gratitude is an *invitation.* It's an opportunity to place our trust and hope in God over anything else we may be experiencing in the moment. Having gone through some intense seasons of suffering in my own life, I know this isn't easy. But perhaps it makes thanksgiving that much more important. When our lives are surrounded by things that don't seem to fit with God's goodness, we can still choose the faith-building act of giving thanks, remembering that as believers we "walk by faith, not by sight" (2 Corinthians 5:7).

Gratitude may not always be something we *feel* but may it always, always be something we *choose.*

Cultivate
Take some time today to personalize those words of 1 Thessalonians 5:18. What situation can you decide to thank God for, even if your feelings don't match up? Find a journal, open up the notes app in your phone or use the space at the back of this book and jot down a prayer, to tell God how even in this you will give him thanks.

3

Opening the Gift

"This is the day that the LORD has made;
let us rejoice and be glad in it."

PSALM 118:24

I woke up early this morning to the news that a dear friend had welcomed a brand-new baby during the night. It was an announcement that was made even more precious because I had been a witness to all that had come before—years of miscarriages, one after another, without any foreseeable end in sight.

We'd cried together, prayed together, shared meals and long afternoon chats, all the while wondering if there would ever be a healthy baby at the end of it all. And now, to be standing in the fulfillment of those dreams… It was hard to imagine anything sweeter.

I promptly sent back a text bursting with excitement, expressing my joy about the new baby and my thanks for a speedy delivery. At the very end, I finished by declaring, "Praise the Lord!" With an exclamation point, of course. As I pressed send, I was reminded of the words of Psalm 118:24:

"This is the day that the LORD has made; let us rejoice and be glad in it." I couldn't think of a more fitting verse for the occasion.

Only recently, our pastor had read those same words at the tail end of a Sunday service, except then, the words hadn't felt so fitting. You see, just the night before, it had snowed. *Again.* And this wasn't December or January or even February. It was straight up April... and still snowing. The snow continued to fall as I ached for sunshine and the chance to start on my garden. Or to do anything that didn't involve bundling up in the protective armor of winter hat, boots, and jacket.

As I stood in church hearing this reminder to *rejoice,* I felt a little bit like a wayward child being reprimanded for my lack of spiritual gratitude. It's natural to rejoice on days that stream with sunshine, bring news of new babies, and serve up situations that make sense. But how could I find joy on the other days? How could I give thanks in the midst of unending miscarriages and busted-up relationships and weather conditions that didn't seem to take any cues from the calendar?

But take note of a key word in verse 24: *"Let* us..." Growing in gratefulness isn't something we sum up with our own strength or try to will-power our way through on our own. But as we've already seen, growing gratefully begins by actively choosing to take God at his word and believe in its truth for our lives.

Friend, I want you to grasp this truth because I believe it holds such freedom for our everyday lives. Gratefulness is simply a gift that God wants us to receive.

What do I mean by that? I mean that when we give thanks, it helps us to see what is, in fact, true.

When we're steeped in our circumstances, it can be easy for our minds to wander from God's truth. But expressing gratitude—giving God thanks—is one of the surest ways in which we can align our lives with his promises. Gratitude means choosing to accept what God says about our circumstances and staking our lives on his promises. It's an opportunity to give our faith footsteps and live in accordance with God's unchanging nature. The call to give thanks doesn't need to trigger feelings of failure or condemnation—it can serve as a beacon calling us back toward what is sure and unchanging.

Gratefulness most certainly is available for us today! It's simply *accepting* what God says—about us and about himself—and stepping forward into the blessed assurance of a life lived in him. We can encourage one another in this, just as the psalmist does.

God's love for us isn't conditional so neither should be our gratitude. God's sovereignty isn't variable so neither should be our thankfulness. God's character isn't circumstantial so neither should be our ability to rejoice and be glad no matter what situations we may be facing.

Giving thanks isn't a burden; it's a blessed reminder of the unshakable truths of our God. May we open up this gift of gratitude and receive his truth once again.

Cultivate
Consider some unchangeable truths about God and the relationship you are able to have with him. Receive them as a gift again today as you turn to thanksgiving and rejoice in his great promises.

4

Everyday Emmanuel

"Where shall I go from your Spirit? Or where shall I flee
from your presence? If I ascend to heaven, you are there!
If I make my bed in Sheol, you are there!"

PSALM 139:7-8

The sound of 180-something shouting kids reverberated against the walls of the church sanctuary. All around me were the sights of a biblical-era city, courtesy of our church's week-long Vacation Bible School program—palm trees, brick walls, even a fountain spouting actual water from a sprinkler set up in the church baptismal.

Each night closed with a tagline based on a biblical truth such as, "When I feel lonely, God is with me" or "When things change, God is with me." But on this particular evening, as the teachers chanted and all the kids raised their voices as one, the depth of those last words struck me—*God is with me*. Surrounded by tissue-paper decorations, stray glo-sticks, and more than a few wiggly bodies paying little attention, I was surprised to find myself fighting back tears as the full weight of those words settled in.

God is with me.

How needed would these words be as the children headed back to varied home lives and challenging school situations and all the confusion of our busted-up world. And how much do you and I need to hear them too?

We often use the name Emmanuel to refer to Jesus during the Christmas season, yet sometimes we forget the depth of this truth in the remaining days of the year. When we face times of difficulty and disappointment, *God is with us.* As we navigate the changes and challenges of a new beginning, *God is with us.* Even while we make our way through the ordinary and everyday, *God is with us.*

John 1:14 reminds us, "And the Word became flesh and dwelt among us, and we have seen his glory, glory as of the only Son from the Father, full of grace and truth." Jesus, whose name literally means *God with us,* left behind his heavenly home to enter our sin-sick world—simply because he wanted a relationship with us.

When I look through the Gospels, I can't escape the fact that so many elements of the Christmas story seem like the wrong time and place—an unwed pregnant teen, a challenging political climate, a last-minute trip without any accommodation, and the list could go on. Still Galatians 4:4 reminds us that "when the fullness of time had come, God sent forth his Son..."

At exactly the right place and exactly the right time, Jesus Christ was born. Through it all, God was orchestrating every tiny detail to work in conjunction and bring about his sovereign plan. Yes, even through messiness and brokenness and things that aren't "just so."

I don't know about you, but this is a truth I so desperately need to be reminded of in my own life—it doesn't need to be perfect in order for God to be present. The words of Psalm 139:7-8 are such a blessed reminder of this truth: "Where shall I go from your Spirit? Or where shall I flee from your presence? If I ascend to heaven, you are there! If I make my bed in Sheol, you are there!" Wherever we go, whatever we go through, God is with us.

I wonder if our problem often isn't that God is distant but that too often we miss him. Is our vision sometimes so clouded by life that we fail to see that God has been beside us the entire time?

This is the real power behind gratitude: that even in the moments when God feels far away and life is just plain hard, it points us back to God's presence. With each breath of praise, in every word of thanks, our hearts are directed back to this truth that *God is with us.*

Growing a grateful heart isn't about us getting all of this down perfectly but about a perfect Savior who *already has hold of us*—one who is loving us and abiding with us through any and every bit of our lives. Whatever you may be facing today, God is present and accessible for you.

Come and dwell in his presence. Thank him for the promise that brokenness is never the end of the story with Jesus.

You're going to be okay. More than okay, actually. You've got God.

Will you pray with me?
Lord, we thank you for the knowledge that no matter what comes our way, you are present. You are constant. And because of that, we know that anything is possible—nothing we face is too broken for your healing hands. God, we pray that you would open our eyes and ears to be more aware of your presence. Help our hearts to be more sensitive to your Spirit working inside us. Most of all, we thank you that we have you. In Jesus' name, Amen.

5

Sweet Surrender

"Give thanks in all circumstances;
for this is the will of God in Christ Jesus for you."

1 THESSALONIANS 5:18

I've shared my trepidation about this verse already, but I just can't ignore the importance of its last phrase—"for this is the will of God in Christ Jesus for you."

Yes, giving thanks itself is God's will for our lives. And yet tucked in this verse is also another important truth—that we can give thanks right in the middle of whatever situation we may find ourselves, trusting that our trials are part of his perfect will too.

Can I be transparent? There has been more than one occasion when I've found this almost impossible to do. I've stared in the face of things which don't seem to hold the slightest ounce of goodness for which I can be thankful. Unexpectedly losing my son. A painful church split. Crushing relationship blows that felt unfixable and even unforgivable.

And I'm guessing that if we were sitting across a table from one another, you could share some similarly challenging circumstances from your own life—maybe financial troubles or a health diagnosis or any number of issues that tug at your heart. How then do we go from merely stumbling through these hard times to actually *growing* through them? How do we not only refuse to give in to the temptation to grumble or grow negative but instead offer God praise?

The answer is simply this—we surrender. Jesus describes it this way in John 12:24: "Unless a grain of wheat falls into the earth and dies, it remains alone; but if it dies, it bears much fruit." In order to bear much fruit, the seed must first die.

Growth can only happen if there is first a death. The process of darkness and waiting is the very thing necessary for the seed to fulfill its purpose—to bear fruit. The burial is a new beginning.

I wonder how many of us have seeds within us that must first die before we can begin growing the good things that God has for our lives? How many of us need to lay down our own dreams and expectations in order to start living the life God has prepared for us?

Scripture tells us that Jesus himself wrestled with this kind of surrendered living. As he tarried in the Garden of Gethsemane on the night before his crucifixion, he prayed, "Father, if you are willing, remove this cup from me. Nevertheless, not my will, but yours, be done" (Luke 22:42).

This was no easy surrender. In fact, Luke 22:44 says that Jesus was in such distress that "his sweat became like great drops of blood falling down to the ground." Nor was it simply a one-and-done surrender, either. Over and over throughout his ministry, Jesus exemplified this kind of laid-down living, telling his followers that he came "...not to do my own will but the will of him who sent me" (John 6:38).

Jesus went through all this suffering in perfect obedience to his Father. How much more do you and I need to confess when we hold onto our own way with an iron fist?

Sometimes surrender *will* feel like a death. It will seem like the ending of our dreams, the funeral of our expectations, the laying down of so many of our plans. But can I promise you this? It will also be a beginning.

Submission can be the birthplace for a brand new life that God has ordained: one that is greater than anything you might have dreamed up yourself. As you repent of grasping tightly to your will and then burying your own expectations, that act of dying to self is exactly what's necessary for you to grow. Just as Jesus' death and burial were necessary for the miracle of the resurrection and our salvation, so the deaths and burials in our own lives are often how God raises us anew.

This is how we can live lives which overflow with gratefulness. This is how we let go of disappointments and refuse to slide into bitterness over the course of our lives. We die to our own will and surrender to his.

Friend, what dreams do you need to lay down in your life today? What disappointments do you need to let go of in order to fully see the beautiful plans God has for you?

Perhaps that thing that felt like an ending is, in fact, a beginning. Maybe the disappointments aren't just a death— rather, they're the fertile ground that God is preparing, ready to bear much fruit.

Will you pray with me?

Lord, sometimes the disappointments I've walked through feel more like endings than beginnings. But Father, will you help me see my life the way you see it? I surrender my dreams and plans and everything I am into your loving hands. Father, thank you that you aren't just burying me; you're bringing new things to life. In Jesus' name, Amen.

Planting the Seeds

SOWING THOUGHTS OF THANKSGIVING

6

Think on These Things

"Finally, brothers, whatever is true, whatever is honorable, whatever is just, whatever is pure, whatever is lovely, whatever is commendable, if there is any excellence, if there is anything worthy of praise, think about these things."

PHILIPPIANS 4:8

I recently started a gratitude journal. Okay, I'm not quite sure that's what you'd call it—it's just a simple notebook from our local dollar store with a slowly growing list of things I'm grateful for—but I started it all the same. I picked up a pen and the notebook and stood at my kitchen counter, trying to ignore the fingerprint smudges, the sporadic scatters of crumbs on the floor, and the ever-growing laundry piles, and I wrote.

Iridescent soap bubbles in the sink.
Sunshine streaming through the kitchen window.
Juicy bites of watermelon that drips down my face.

It sounded slightly silly at first. A bit trivial. Maybe even a little forced. But before I knew it, the list started to grow longer.

Little hands to teach and train.
The grace and forgiveness found in Christ.
The freedom to live in a country where I can worship freely.

And I slowly began to realize: I can choose what I see. Let me pause and repeat that so we can both let the words soak down deep. We can *choose* what we see.

We can choose to see the good and the beautiful even when life feels bad and ugly. We can choose to take in what is true and right even when we're surrounded by things that seem absolutely wrong. We can decide for ourselves that despite all the messiness and madness in our world, we are going to focus our hearts and minds on what is God-honoring and glorifying to Christ.

Philippians 4:8 reminds us, "Whatever is honorable, whatever is just, whatever is pure, whatever is lovely, whatever is commendable, if there is any excellence, if there is anything worthy of praise, think about these things."

Notice those last words: *think about these things.* Not try or attempt or give it your best shot, but just a simple command to ponder on all that is lovely.

I have to be careful with what I let influence my spirit. I have to be intentional with what takes up my time, my attention, and my heart. In my own life, that means being cautious with the kind of media and even news I allow in, otherwise I'll find myself sucked into a downward cycle of doom and discouragement. Maybe you'll find you need to evaluate some of those spaces in your own life too.

Because, friend, I've discovered that giving thanks is the most tangible way of applying those words of Philippians 4:8 every day. Expressing gratitude is how we focus our minds on what is good and pure. Praising God is how we remind our hearts of what is true and eternally unchanging. Glorifying God with our words is how we focus our spiritual eyes on those things that are "excellent or praiseworthy" and away from the things that try to distract us or bring us down.

No, this doesn't mean that the mess in our lives will magically disappear. I can't tell you how many times in the day I find myself confronted with a sibling squabble or a moody teen or another mountain of laundry, but now I also see something else: gifts.

Gifts of everyday goodness. Gifts of grace right in the midst of the hard. Gifts that I might otherwise have missed if my eyes weren't focused on the greater story of God's truth and grace.

This takes faith. Sometimes the gifts in our lives aren't readily apparent. And yet isn't that the very essence of faith itself? *Choosing* to see what God says and then to live our lives in accordance rather basing everything on what we may see around us.

So, I'll keep jotting entries in my journal, scribbling down glimpses of goodness and focusing my heart on truth. I'm not so easily burdened when my eyes are turned to what is just and pure and lovely. I'm going to think on these things.

Cultivate

Take a personal inventory of the things you're filling up on today—news, social media, television, even your music selections. Which of those could you replace with what is true and pure and lovely that will fill you with thanks?

7

Sowing the Right Seeds

*"We destroy arguments and every lofty opinion raised
against the knowledge of God, and take every thought
captive to obey Christ."*

2 CORINTHIANS 10:5

One unexpectedly wonderful thing that came out of those
slow, locked-down days of the pandemic was starting
my garden. During those early days of seclusion, we began
researching, reading about various methods, and—most
importantly—planning what we actually wanted to plant.

We dreamed of large, juicy cucumbers and bright tomatoes
to can for the winter. We envisioned fresh salads of spinach
greens and kale and handfuls of raspberries plucked straight
from our own bushes. And so we tilled the soil and added
heaps of compost and planted those tiny slivers of seeds in the
hope that in only a few short months (or maybe even less) we
might be eating the literal fruits of our labor.

Whether it's visions of fruit and vegetables or a dream of
becoming more contented and thankful, we all want to grow
good things in our lives. And yet, how often do we think

about what we are *actually planting* in the soil of our hearts?

The seeds that are being sown through the things we think about are powerful—because what we dwell on *does* matter. 2 Corinthians 10:5 encourages us to "demolish arguments and every pretension that sets itself up against the knowledge of God, and we take captive every thought to make it obedient to Christ" (NIV).

Why is God concerned about our thought life? Because our thoughts, when left unchecked, will grow into beliefs, which will soon develop into the way we live our lives.

I'll admit that for far too long I've been an unconscious cultivator of my heart. I've allowed myself to become a victim of fleeting feelings and flighty thoughts, never realizing I had a choice in what kind of seeds I was planting. Will I give in to every thought and feeling that drops into my heart? Or will I instead grab hold of the truth of God's word and plant those seeds in my heart, trusting in its sufficiency for my life?

This is why cultivating grateful thoughts is so vital to our vibrancy as Christians. As we actively immerse ourselves in God's word and choose to apply its truth to our lives, we can bring our thoughts into obedience to God through the act of giving him thanks—planting those good seeds which will lead to a more abundant life in him.

Colossians 3:2 encourages us to "set our minds on things that are above, not on things that are on earth." Friend, have you paid attention to what kinds of seeds are being planted in the soil of your mind today? Are they thoughts of the "things that are above" or are you being dragged down by earthly things that are "[setting themselves] up against the knowledge of God" (2 Corinthians 10:5)? Take these destructive thoughts captive through the truth of Scripture and, instead, captivate your heart by dwelling on all that he has set before you. As we thank Jesus for his unchanging character and praise him in agreement with what his word says, our hearts are being planted with seeds that will bloom into gratitude and contentment.

The garden of your heart is sacred ground. Your life is meant to reap a bountiful harvest filled with praise. And it all begins by planting good seeds.

Cultivate

Today I want you to actively consider the seeds that are being planted in the soil of your heart. What are those areas where you've been finding your thought-life drawn away from Christ? As you contemplate those areas, take those thoughts captive through the act of thanksgiving and let God sow the seeds of his truth in your heart.

8

A Heart of Praise

"Great are the works of the LORD,
studied by all who delight in them.
Full of splendor and majesty is his work,
and his righteousness endures forever.
He has caused his wondrous works to be remembered;
the LORD is gracious and merciful."

PSALM 111:2-4

I dug my phone out from my back pocket and set it heavily down on the counter, music still blaring. It had been one of those days where the worship music had been on constantly, trying to drown out the spiraling thoughts and nagging worries that were threatening to take over my mind. I couldn't seem to *think,* much less *pray.*

And so I'd walked. Or perhaps a more accurate description might be, I'd paced. Wandering from one room to the next, picking up strewn-about toys and discarded books, all the while trying to override the whispers of doubt with words of praise.

It didn't happen all at once but, slowly and quietly, the worry began to lift. Over time, the fears felt further away; the darkness seemed less tangible, and hope began to seep back into my heart again.

Friend, I believe this is the faith-building power of giving God praise. In those moments when we most need it—and perhaps least feel it—God is beckoning us to bring him praise. Putting truth on our lips through a song of praise is a powerful way that we can cement our hearts and minds on God's truth.

Psalm 111:2-4 tells us, "How amazing are the deeds of the LORD! All who delight in him should ponder them. Everything he does reveals his glory and majesty. His righteousness never fails. He causes us to remember his wonderful works. How gracious and merciful is our LORD!" (NLT).

God prompts us to truly stop and ponder his amazing deeds because he knows that doing so will shift our focus. In fact, he tells us that it is he who "causes us to remember his wonderful works" and that this should point us toward how "gracious and merciful" our God is. Praising God is what's best for *us*.

Over and over as I study gratitude in Scripture, I'm struck by how often thanksgiving and praise are intertwined, so much so that they're nearly impossible to separate. And I've noticed this same thing in my own life.

Maybe I'm having a hard day where I'm feeling down and the words of a worship song point me right back to what's true. Or I'm at a church service when a hymn I've heard a hundred times strikes me right in the core. This is why praise is so powerful—it directs our eyes away from our situation and shifts them back to the Savior.

Sometimes this will most certainly cost us something. Hebrews 13:15 tells us, "Through him then let us continually offer up a sacrifice of praise to God, that is, the fruit of lips that acknowledge his name." Praise won't necessarily feel like something that makes sense or chimes with what we're experiencing.

But can I share the best part? It most certainly won't cost us anything we truly want to keep. It may cost us our fear, but it will grow our faith deeper. It may cost us our despair, but it will increase our joy. It may cost us our pride, but it will reveal to us a greater view of the limitless depths of Christ's love.

Because praise reminds us most of all that what God says is *true*. Praise points us straight back to God's presence. And fear and anxiety simply can't stick around wherever our God is.

In the words of Colossians 3:16, let's be people who choose the power of praise: "Let the word of Christ dwell in you richly, teaching and admonishing one another in all wisdom, singing psalms and hymns and spiritual songs, with thankfulness in your hearts to God." Are you ready to offer up a sacrifice of praise that plants you right back on the rock-solid footing of Jesus?

Let the word of Christ dwell in you richly through the power of giving God praise.

Cultivate

Turn on some worship music and simply spend some time praising God for who he is and what he's done in your life.

9

Suffering from Spiritual Amnesia

"Bless the LORD, O my soul, and forget not all his benefits, who forgives all your iniquity, who heals all your diseases, who redeems your life from the pit, who crowns you with steadfast love and mercy."

PSALM 103:2-4

Recently I was watching an episode of *The Chosen* when an unusual sight caught my attention: Mary Magdalene busily constructing a tent of sorts out of branches and leaves.

Ordinarily this might have passed me by without much notice, except that just that morning I'd been reading this exact passage from Leviticus 23. "You shall dwell in booths for seven days. All native Israelites shall dwell in booths, that your generations may know that I made the people of Israel dwell in booths when I brought them out of the land of Egypt" (v 42-43).

I'd stumbled upon this passage prior but never before had I actually considered the implications of it. Men, women, the elderly, even young children—all living together in makeshift dwellings out in the elements for more than a week. Can you imagine? Everyone pausing their normal routines and daily activities to gather for this one, solitary purpose: *to remember.*

The Feast of Tabernacles—or Festival of Booths, as it is sometimes called—was specifically designed to remind the Israelites of God's supernatural deliverance out of Egypt while also pointing them toward the future return of the Messiah. And this certainly wasn't the only celebration with such ends. Passover, Pentecost, Hanukkah, the Day of Atonement—the Jewish calendar is scattered with festivals and feasts whose sole goal is to point the people of Israel toward remembering what God has done.

I can't help but think how important these reminders are for our own lives. Just take for consideration the sacraments of baptism or communion. Through the physical act of immersion in water, we are reminded of our own death to sin and how we've been raised to new life in Christ. In communion, as we taste the bread and drink from the cup, we experience the tangible memorial of the body that was broken and the blood that was spilled for our salvation.

Without these reminders, it can be all too easy for us to slide into periods of forgetfulness. That's why verses like Psalm 103:2-4 encourage us with these words: "Praise the LORD, my soul, and forget not all his benefits—who forgives all your sins and heals all your diseases, who redeems your life from the pit and crowns you with love and compassion" (NIV).

So how can we avoid slipping into these moments of spiritual memory lapse in our everyday lives? How can we not fall prey to forgetting the great things God has done?

We actively choose the way of remembering through giving God thanks.

When you're feeling the weight of your failure, you thank God and remember that he "forgives all your sins." When you're struggling under a burden that feels like it's about ready to bury you, you thank God and remember that he is the one who "redeems your life from the pit." When you're faced with situations that seem senseless, you thank God and remember that he "crowns you with love and compassion."

The real power behind remembering is that when we reflect on God's faithfulness *before,* we are reminded that he will be faithful *again.* These past illustrations of God's faithfulness can serve as powerful examples that God will continue to be exactly who he says he is, yesterday, today, and forever. Such evidence can grow within us an unshakable sense of peace, an unchanging foundation of faith, and an unstoppable hold of hope.

Friend, let's be believers who refuse to succumb to the slide of forgetfulness. Let's choose to look back at our lives and see that God has been faithful. God has been good. God has been present. And the more we look, the more I promise we'll see.

This is the power of our *remembering.*

Cultivate

Take a moment to reflect on God's faithfulness to you in the past—maybe looking back at calendar dates of significant moments in your faith journey, such as a baptism or conversion experience, big prayers that have been answered or memorable milestones where you've seen God grow your faith. Add them to your calendar for the upcoming year to celebrate those past moments of faithfulness in your present.

Putting Down Roots

**DEEPENING GRATITUDE FROM
HEAD TO HEART**

10

In the Vine

"Let your roots grow down into him, and let your lives be built on him. Then your faith will grow strong in the truth you were taught, and you will overflow with thankfulness."

COLOSSIANS 2:7 (NLT)

Last year, my husband and I went to a marriage conference. In all honesty, the years leading up to this had been rife with challenges. Navigating loss, encountering major life changes, not to mention the tensions and turmoil of everyday life—all these things had begun to take their toll.

As speakers shared their stories and we chatted with several other couples, one message stood out above all else: marriage takes intentionality. One of our handouts showed a graphic for this, illustrating two sticks thrown together in a moving current, naturally drifting apart. Similarly, the outside forces in our lives—jobs and finances and even our own families—can pull apart a marriage relationship unless we're intentional about keeping it together.

And in much the same way, it takes intentionality to grow gratefully. We won't simply fall into gratefulness or accidentally find ourselves increasing in joy. Growing gratefully requires an intentional decision to stay connected to Christ. No, not by working on ourselves or focusing on all the things we can do but simply and solely by continuing to remain in him.

Notice these words from John 15:4 as Jesus reminds us, "Abide in me, and I in you. As the branch cannot bear fruit by itself, unless it abides in the vine, neither can you, unless you abide in me."

This is the key. This is the source for any fruitfulness and every bit of growth: *abiding*. It's entirely impossible for us to grow anything spiritually good in our lives by ourselves. The only way we can develop fruits such as peace or joy is by being connected to Jesus Christ as our source.

As believers, our job isn't growing—it's *abiding*.

And isn't that the message of the gospel? Just as Christ is the only one who accomplished and completed our salvation on the cross, so our sanctification is complete only in him, as well. That's just a fancier way of saying that Jesus is the one who makes us look like him. Colossians 2:7 tells us, "Let your roots grow down into him, and let your lives be built on him. Then your faith will grow strong in the truth you were taught, and you will overflow with thankfulness" (NLT).

Did you catch that? Not just an occasional word of gratitude that's circumstantial or conditional but a life literally overflowing with it! Don't you want to live that kind of life?

I'm so encouraged by this because, yes, while we need to be intentional about staying connected to Jesus, this is *all we need to do*. We can allow God to do the work *he* needs to do in our hearts to form us into strong people of faith. We can lead lives overflowing with gratefulness because our foundation isn't what we're seeing or how we're feeling—it's rooted in a faith that's sunk down deep in Christ.

In the New Living Translation, 2 Peter 1:35 reminds us to "make every effort to respond to God's promises." Notice the dichotomy here. God's promises are *already* ours, yet we are instructed to "make every effort" to respond to them.

And why is this? It's because our response to God's promises—our willingness to remain in him—allows us to reap the benefits of a life firmly established on Christ. Our work is simply to stay connected to Christ's finished work.

Growing strong and overflowing with thanks isn't about our own ability; it's about God's.

Cultivate

Here's my challenge to you today. Take one of your normal, everyday habits—eating breakfast, taking a shower, even brushing your teeth—and spend those moments silently (or outwardly!) reflecting on what it means to abide in Jesus. Thank him for his finished work on the cross and for the grace he's poured out on us to just receive.

11

The Slow Grow

*"For thus said the Lord God, the Holy One of Israel,
'In returning and rest you shall be saved; in quietness
and in trust shall be your strength.'"*

ISAIAH 30:15

"You can *slow down.*"

The softly spoken words coming from the side of the room startled me out of my rush. I had been in the middle of washing my hands—hurriedly—when this sentence, spoken by a fellow bathroom-visitor, caught me by surprise.

"Oh... I know," I sheepishly admitted, barely catching her eye before hastily ripping off a section of paper towel. "I have four kids waiting for me outside."

Her seasoned eyes smiled at me as she watched while I dried my hands. "They'll be alright. You just take the time you need."

I smiled in amusement, still half-sprinting out of the bathroom. She didn't get it, I figured. Maybe she didn't have little ones or had forgotten what it was like to be constantly in demand.

Now, being chided by a stranger for my hurriedness was a bit unusual, but being in a rush had become fairly routine. Often, I'd find myself becoming impatient or anxious, hurried and hassled yet still wondering whether I was really accomplishing anything that mattered. And I was steadily growing more short with the people and frustrated with the places right in front of me—all in the grand name of productivity and efficiency.

The reality was beginning to sink in—*living in a hurry only left me with a heart that was equally hurried.*

These words from Isaiah 30:15 have been such a challenge to me in this quest toward decelerating my own hurried heart and taking time for thanksgiving. Here, God himself reminds us that, "In returning and rest you shall be saved; in quietness and in trust shall be your strength."

So often I'm tempted to think that if only I can accomplish more or produce faster or work just a little bit harder, I'll have a life of value and worth that I can be grateful for. But here God is reminding us that real strength comes from our quietness and trust in him. And deliverance? It's found when we rest in what he's already done.

I wonder if sometimes all our yearning to lead a life that truly matters (a desire that I believe was placed within us by God himself) can be twisted so that we believe we'll miss out unless we chase harder and hustle more. Maybe too often we end up settling for lives that are productive over purposeful, and efficient instead of actually effective for the kingdom of God.

If you too have struggled with being a hurrier, I want to encourage you today that nothing you can do will make God love you any more or any less. You are already a beloved child of the King. Slow down and rest in what Christ has already done.

A meaningful life isn't something we need to chase after to feel fulfilled; fulfillment is found in chasing after someone who loves us more than anyone else ever could. Jesus' first words to several of his disciples allude to this fact as he beckons them, "Come, follow me" (Luke 18:22).

This is where we find true meaning and purpose for our lives—in following Christ. He is the one who sets the pace. With him leading, we can live fully present in our todays, not race ahead of all of their goodness in search for tomorrows that we can never quite grasp.

We'll miss out on most moments of gratefulness if we're in too much of a hurry to truly notice them. Early morning sunshine, a hot drink to greet the day, a plate of food to fill our bellies? All of these seemingly ordinary gifts are really anything but—when we truly stop to take them in.

I'm convinced that when we slow down, we'll soon begin to discover that a fruitful and gratifying life isn't found in what we can accomplish but in knowing the one who has accomplished it all on the cross. Real purpose and meaning aren't goals we have to chase but gifts that already belong to us. Sometimes, we just need to slow down enough to really see them and to fully accept God's enoughness with quiet thanks.

Are you looking for meaning? Are you chasing after what really matters? Are you ready to stop living in a hurry and start gratefully embracing the life God has given you?

To this Jesus simply says, "Come, follow me."

Cultivate

What is something that you usually rush through in the day? How could you can actively choose to slow down instead and savor the life God has given you?

12

Pulling up Weeds

"So we see that they were unable to enter because of unbelief."

HEBREWS 3:19

I added a new, recurring task in my phone's calendar: weed my garden.

The first year we'd started out the weeds weren't so bad. The plot was small and easily managed with a few pulled up handfuls during a routine visit to water or gather harvests. But as we'd grown and expanded our space, these unwanted and unexpected visitors had snuck their way in, sucking up nutrients out of the soil and making for a rather unsightly mess. We hadn't planted them or desired for them, yet here they were.

Doesn't that pattern sound familiar? We start out expectant for growth and excited to experience all the good things God has planned. We have hopes and dreams for how fruitful our lives should now be looking—only to find any growth seemingly choked out by the pressures of the world around us, and our thankfulness waning.

Jesus describes four types of soil in Matthew 13: the hard path, the rocky soil, the thorny ground, and the good soil. And while the first two soils are described as being unfit for growth, the interesting thing about the third is that it isn't the soil itself that's the problem—it's the things that sprout up within it.

Jesus explains this, saying, "As for what was sown among thorns, this is the one who hears the word, but the cares of the world and the deceitfulness of riches choke the word, and it proves unfruitful" (Matthew 13:22).

Gulp. I can't be the only one who endeavors to live a thankful life, yet often ends up unexpectedly burdened by the cares of the world or tempted by the ease and allure of the good life.

I don't think any of us intentionally stunt good growth in our own lives, yet how many of us fail to recognize that the real root of weeds is *unbelief?* Whether we're fighting the temptation to take the path of an easier life or feeling burdened by our troubles, we unknowingly cultivate these thorns whenever we fail to live in thankful trust of God.

Just take the case of the Israelites. Growing up in Sunday school, I remember often hearing stories about their grumbling journey through the wilderness. And frankly, I couldn't help but feel a bit frustrated with these people. Didn't they remember what God had just done for them? How could they already have forgotten how he'd parted seas and destroyed armies and miraculously rained down food from heaven for them?

Somehow all that desert sand had disintegrated their faith into streams of complaining. In fact, Scripture tells us that the people actually wished they were dead! In Exodus 16:3, they declare to Moses, "Would that we had died by the hand of the LORD in the land of Egypt, when we sat by the meat pots and ate bread to the full."

Suddenly the Israelites are looking back on Egypt not as the root of their bondage and the source of all their suffering but as the place where they'd "sat by the meat pots and ate bread to the full." What is going on?

Take a look now at what Hebrews 3:15-19 has to say about the Israelites: "Who were they who heard and rebelled? Were they not all those Moses led out of Egypt? And with whom was he angry for forty years? Was it not with those who sinned, whose bodies perished in the wilderness? And to whom did God swear that they would never enter his rest if not to those who disobeyed? So we see that they were not able to enter, because of their unbelief."

The Israelites were caught up in all the cares of this life. They were deceived into looking back on their past with some seriously rose-colored glasses—and traded out a rich relationship of trust with their Savior for the tempting allure of a life of ease. Their grumbling simply revealed what was buried down in their hearts: *unbelief.*

How can we look out for these weeds coming up in our own lives? *We pay attention to those areas where we find it easier to grumble than to give thanks.* What are the untruths that we are believing about God's character? In what areas of your life is it a struggle to trust God?

Living a thankful life is far easier when the soil of your soul is cultivated by trust in your Father. As he makes you aware of any weeds in your own life, ask for forgiveness. Confess any areas of unbelief and let your heart and mind be renewed through the truth of God's word. There's no better way to rid our lives of the weeds of this world than through thanksgiving.

Cultivate

Carefully observe the things you speak about today. Are they words of dissatisfaction or protesting or nitpicking? Prayerfully ask God to reveal any areas where you are struggling with believing him, and for specific Scriptures to meditate on to build your faith.

13

So Long Fear

"Blessed is the man who trusts in the LORD,
whose trust is the LORD."

JEREMIAH 17:7

Sometimes I struggle with fear. And not just teeny, tiny fears that I can reason my way out of but huge, heavy ones that feel like nothing good is standing in my future and everything in my world is ready to swallow me whole. Because, to speak plainly, as a mother who's experienced the loss of a child, I've stood in the face of some of my own worst fears. But can I share with you a little of what I've discovered?

God was there too.

In the middle of my worst nightmares, God was right there beside me, strengthening me with unexplainable peace, carrying me through those moments when I didn't think I could go one step farther. Even during my absolute worst, God sustained me.

Jeremiah describes this so beautifully, using the metaphor of a tree to demonstrate how trusting God grows deep roots in our lives that will sustain us no matter what may come. Verse 7 of chapter 17 tells us, "Blessed is the man who trusts in the LORD, whose trust is the LORD. He is like a tree planted by water, that sends out its roots by the stream, and does not fear when heat comes, for its leaves remain green, and is not anxious in the year of drought, for it does not cease to bear fruit."

What a wonderful promise! When our trust is in God, our lives will be like a tree that is planted by a river of ever-running water. We don't have to fear what's coming next or even be anxious in the fiery or dry times in life. In fact, it says that through it all, we will *prosper.* Isn't that the kind of confidence you want?

Maybe you're wondering, how in the world do I go about doing this in any practical sense?

When I'm hit by these moments that send my mind spinning and my heart beating, underneath the surface I've begun letting my fear of my situation overshadow my fear of God. Instead of placing my faith in him and being sustained by that river of love, I'm placing my confidence in all the things going on around me. Fear is simply misdirected faith.

But the fastest way to turn your fear into faith is by giving God thanks.

And so, I began to bring those fears to the feet of Jesus— financial struggles, scary health unknowns, issues with my kids, whatever they may be—and I imagine him standing right there, in whatever I'm facing. As I picture him in all his gentleness and all his glory, I praise my Savior, thanking him for how he's shown himself to be faithful before and how he will do so again.

And you know what begins to happen? The darkness and the doubts start to shrink and instead I rest in the arms of a Savior who loves me and promises to use everything for my good and for his glory—even the things that scare me.

How I wish I could promise you that nothing fearful or anxiety-inducing would ever happen in your future! But instead, I can promise you this—*God will be there.* He'll be the one gently guiding you, holding you close, and drawing you near, no matter what the future may bring. We don't need to walk through life handcuffed by all the unknowns. Instead we can give God thanks, shooting out roots further and deeper into the streams of his goodness, with the knowledge that his love won't ever run dry.

We will find we are steady and solid when we are planted on him. Fear and anxiety begin to loosen their grip. The leaves of our lives stay green, and even more than that, show signs of fruitfulness. Not through our own strength or ability but simply because *God is our source.*

Cultivate

As you are confronted with moments of worry or fear today or this week, I want to encourage you to do two things. First imagine Jesus in the middle of whatever you're facing. Then as you envision him there beside you, actively thank him—for who he is, for his goodness and faithfulness to you, for the ways he's provided for you before, and how he promises to do so in the future. And watch as he grows your faith in him to be bigger than your fear of anything else.

14

Thanks-Fueled Prayer

*"Do not be anxious about anything, but in everything
by prayer and supplication with thanksgiving let your
requests be made known to God. And the peace of God,
which surpasses all understanding, will guard your hearts
and your minds in Christ Jesus."*

PHILIPPIANS 4:6-7

I recently confided to a friend that I've been finding it hard
to pray. There's been a situation going on in my life that
doesn't just feel like a thorn—it's more like a log in my side.
And I've prayed and cried and practically begged God to
change it and to intervene, except the situation stays the same.
And sometimes it even looks like it's getting worse.

This friend invited me to a park to pray earlier this month.
And during our time together, I was suddenly struck by the
truth: the reason why I was finding it hard to pray was because
I was angry with God. Instead of praying for *thy* will, I had
subconsciously been praying for *my* will—for God to do
things in the way and timing that I thought was best rather
than in his way.

I've so needed the words of Philippians 4:6: "Don't worry about anything, but in all your prayers ask God for what you need, always asking him with a thankful heart" (GNT).

If you're anything like me, you have no problem asking God for the things you need. To be honest, my prayer time too often sounds like a laundry list of all the things in my world that I think should be fixed or changed in some way.

But dwelling on this verse made me recognize something: *without thanksgiving, prayer can tend to be all about me.* And while God certainly does love to hear our prayers and requests, the transformative power of thanksgiving is essential for raising our vision beyond everything that we think needs fixing.

Notice the radical shift that takes place when we pepper our prayers with this kind of thankfulness. Verse 7 goes on to say, "And God's peace, which is far beyond human understanding, will keep your hearts and minds safe in union with Christ Jesus" (GNT).

God's peace is accessible to us *through thanksgiving.* When we acknowledge his presence in our lives in this way, we are actually inviting God's supernatural peace into our hearts. When we discover the posture of gratitude, peace that goes "beyond human understanding" is ours right in the middle of those situations that don't seem to make any sense.

Friend, I want you to know that I write this not because I've figured the whole thing out or that I'm somehow further ahead on this journey—I write it because this is what I so desperately need in my own heart. Giving God thanks doesn't always come easily—but it beats the alternative of living in frustration or resentment for the way things are. I don't want to live for my own will; I want to live for God's.

So will you join me? Are you ready to lay down your own will so that you can accept with thankfulness what God has given you right now?

As you come to God with your requests and worries for the day, begin by giving him thanks. Let him keep your heart and mind safe through the power of thanksgiving. Pepper your prayers with praise and find how union with Christ and living for his will combats the bewilderment and bitterness that can come with living for your own ways.

Prayer is powerful not only because our heavenly Father is bending his ear to us but also because we are bending our ears *to him*. Ultimately prayer is for us but it isn't about us. It's about God's will being done on earth as it is in heaven—and may it start in our hearts.

Cultivate

As you come to God in prayer for what you need today, sandwich each request with a prayer of thanks. If you need some help getting started, open up your Bible to Psalm 34 or Psalm 100 and personalize those words of praise.

15

Contentment

*"Not that I am speaking of being in need, for I have
learned in whatever situation I am to be content."*

PHILIPPIANS 4:11

I invited a new friend over to our house for the first
time with her kids. And I just couldn't get over how
appreciative she was. "What a cute decorating style! Oh,
I love those curtains. You really have a beautiful piece of
property here."

As I listened to her compliments, inside I felt this little
twinge of guilt because I knew in my heart that I hadn't been
the most grateful about our home. In fact, just a year before
I'd begun insisting to my husband that we needed to remodel
our kitchen or finish the back yard or just plain *move*. So
much so that I'd finally convinced him to meet up with a
realtor to check out a lot a few miles south of us.

Oh, how I could envision us there! I could see our children
rambling around the forest and scampering up trees and us all
enjoying the bright, fresh amenities of a brand new house. I
could imagine it all… *except the price tag.*

And so we stayed in the old home. As the year progressed, I began wrestling with this idea of contentment. How could I choose contentment while facing so many things that I couldn't change? And what did it actually look like to live this out in my everyday life?

I decided to plant roots—both literally and figuratively. After a long time of debating back and forth with myself, I finally went ahead and ordered fruit trees. Next, I started a garden chock-full of carrots and rhubarb, and planted bare-root raspberries to begin my own patch. I even got chickens!

I'm not saying that these are the kinds of things you need to do in order to be content. In fact, I don't believe there's a need for us to make major adjustments to our circumstances to alter how we feel about them. What I *am* saying is that we can actively grow in contentment: we can stop dwelling on what *isn't* and embrace what *is*.

So I told God, "If this is where you have me, I'm going to live life fully right where I am. I'm going to quit waiting around for the next season, and instead start embracing and thanking you for where you've placed me. I'm choosing to be present and purposeful and look for the positives in this season. God, as long as you *keep* me here, I'm going to *be* here."

Maybe in your own life that will look like living purposefully while you wait for a season of singleness to end or as you navigate a health condition that's stuck around a whole lot longer than you'd been envisioning. Or maybe it looks like simply embracing the ups and downs of your everyday life and remembering that God is ever present.

Friend, I know that on some days it's easier to do this than on others. I still have moments when I struggle with comparing or simply wishing something would speed up a bit. But real, soul-deep contentment that leads to gratitude isn't found in a certain set of circumstances—it's found in Christ.

Paul sums it up best when he tells us in Philippians 4:11, "Not that I am speaking of being in need, for I have learned in whatever situation I am to be content."

Now this isn't coming from someone simply facing a less than ideal housing arrangement or a minor life inconvenience—he was in prison! Just a few verses later he describes these situations as times of "plenty and hunger, abundance and need." Yet Paul clues us in on the secret behind this contentment: "I can do all things through him who strengthens me" (v 13).

Maybe, like me, you've heard that verse before but never actually stopped to consider the context. I used to think it was referring to the great things we could do for the kingdom of God through the power of Christ, and while that is one aspect we can take from this passage, perhaps the deeper meaning is about what we can *endure*.

Through Christ, we can accept our unchosen circumstances, our less than ideal situations, and even the really heavy things of life, knowing that they first must come through the hands of our loving Father.

Contentment comes from recognizing that whatever circumstance God has us in—whether loss or loneliness or daily challenges—we can thank God because he's in it with us. Contentment is less about what *we* do and more about what *Christ* wants to do in us.

The most beautiful thing we can do? *Embrace it.*

Cultivate

Consider the things in your life *right now.* Spend some time giving God praise for where he has you, for the circumstances you find yourself in, and for how he never changes in both the good and the bad of your messy, ordinary life.

16

Taste and See

"Oh, taste and see that the LORD is good!
Blessed is the man who takes refuge in him!"

PSALM 34:8

The sunlight was streaming through the trees, casting pockets of light across the top of the driveway as I headed out to our garden. My three-year-old toddled along behind, a bucket slung from one hand as she clomped along in her favorite pair of purple rain boots. My other three children were already scampering about in various degrees of helpfulness.

As I looked around that morning, I found myself surprised by a sudden wave of gratitude. It wasn't that life had been easy lately. Quite the opposite, in fact. We'd been going through an extremely painful time with one of our children and it had left me feeling very bleak and burdened. I'd been trudging through the days, trying to tackle the next task at hand without considering much else. But somewhere in all that hand-to-the-plow mentality, I'd been missing *this*.

As I stood there, taking in the sweet sight of my children working outside, the gentle breeze blowing against my face, and the simple goodness of homegrown raspberries, I couldn't escape it—I was surrounded by God's blessings. Yes, even in the midst of a season that felt really hard and heavy, my Savior was inviting me to experience his goodness.

That's the heart behind Psalm 34:8 as it reminds us that even in fear and hardship we can "taste and see that the LORD is good!" Yes, in a spiritual sense this means that we experience the goodness in God's character and what he has achieved for us, but what would it look like if we also applied this in a physical way? What if we stopped to consider the Lord's goodness through our God-gifted senses of taste and sight and sound and smell and touch? Might we more deeply experience God's goodness? Might we develop a keener awareness of his presence?

When we smell the aroma of a home-baked loaf of bread wafting from the oven—*oh, taste and see that the LORD is good!* When we glimpse the myriad colors of an evening sunset— *oh, taste and see that the LORD is good!* When we touch the baby-soft skin of a friend's new little one—*oh, taste and see that the LORD is good!*

Sometimes it's easy to miss these everyday glimpses of God's goodness. So how can you awaken your senses to God's presence when life feels anything but peaceful and put together?

The tail end of Psalm 34:8 gives us the prescription for just that, reminding us, "Blessed is the man who takes refuge in him!" Or in the NKJV, "Blessed is the man who trusts in Him!"

Are you looking for a place of rest and peace? A place of refuge and solace from the cares of this world? Have you been longing for a deeper appreciation and awareness of God's goodness in your life? Taste and see what a good refuge our God is.

Even further, it says we are *blessed.* Seeking and acknowledging God's presence through our sights and smells and sounds leads to a deeper trust and acknowledgment of Christ. Deciding to "taste and see" that the Lord is good reminds us that we have a rock-solid refuge where we can rest from the cares and worries of this world. In Jesus we have a refuge that won't ever fail or falter or leave us longing for more. What a blessing that is!

Friend, I want to challenge you today to pause for a moment and look at all the goodness that surrounds you. Take in the new morning's sunrise; savor those first few bites of breakfast; breathe deep and let God's grace fill up your lungs; whisper words of praise for all the people and gifts he's bestowed upon your life.

And taste and see that the Lord, he *is* good.

Cultivate

As you go about your day, take stock of the good things you experience with your five senses. Thank God for the music playing through the car or even the sound of traffic as you make your way to work. Thank him for the sight of a familiar clerk at the store or a neighbor across the street. Which senses can point you toward more deeply experiencing God's goodness in your life?

17

In the Waiting

"But they who wait for the LORD shall renew their strength;
they shall mount up with wings like eagles; they shall run
and not be weary; they shall walk and not faint."

ISAIAH 40:31

I was sitting in a waiting room—a typical hospital room with bland wallpaper and sterilized seat cushions and the eerie dings of heart rate monitors interspersing the sound of shuffling doctors' feet. It wasn't where I'd expected to be.

This was a day that I'd been planning for *weeks*. Months ago, when grandparents had asked about taking the kids for a weekend, I'd been a little giddy with anticipation. An *entire* day alone in my own house? I'd been dreaming of quiet, uninterrupted moments and all the projects I could get done.

And it had started out rather idyllically: early devotion time curled up on the couch, then quietly starting to check off the chore list; I'd even managed to throw a pan of banana bread into the oven for breakfast. That's when I realized my husband wasn't just sleeping in—he wasn't able to get up for work.

He had thrown out his back the day before and, after a night trying to rest it off, it most definitely was not getting better. So now here we were, sitting in a waiting room with all those plans and projects tossed to the side and more frustration welling up within me than I cared to admit.

No one ever asks to be in a waiting room, and yet there are times in each of our lives where we find ourselves in these spaces—waiting, wondering, and questioning whether the good things we've planted will ever begin to grow. How then do we face these seasons, not with frustration but with faith? How do we wait contentedly and even gratefully, trusting and believing that God is going to do what he said he would do? Not just to wait but to wait *well?*

Isaiah 40:31 tells us, "But they who wait for the LORD shall renew their strength; they shall mount up with wings like eagles; they shall run and not be weary; they shall walk and not faint."

Quite a different view of waiting, isn't it? Here we're told that those who wait on the Lord won't find themselves sapped of strength but instead will be renewed and restored. These people aren't worn out or weary but have actually grown stronger, simply because of this: they've found the source.

I witnessed the same phenomenon in our garden. After all the research and the laborious process of tilling and planting, we did something else. *We waited.*

And slowly, delicately, the plants sprouted. Small tendrils of radish leaves and sprays of spinach greens and the tender leaves of raspberry bushes began to burst forth from the earth in miraculous shades of bright green life.

Here's what I began to realize during those early days of gardening: big things were happening in our waiting. All the silence and seeming nothingness was necessary for the plants to grow roots. In the quiet, dark spaces, these plants were growing the systems and structure necessary to sustain life and stand upright for the outward growth they would soon be ready to show the world.

Similarly God is growing us in our waiting seasons. He's using this time to replace our strength with his own and grow in us a firm foundation that is based on him alone. When our hope is planted in Christ, we will be renewed and rejuvenated through the knowledge that we're not dependent on ourselves—we're rooted in Christ.

We can renew our strength and align our lives with the truth by thanking God right in the middle of the wait. We praise him, even when our dreams feel buried and our growth looks impossible—believing that, with him as our source, we will mount up with wings like eagles over the seemingly insurmountable situations of life.

Friend, if the idea of anything worthwhile growing in your season of waiting feels foreign or far away, can I whisper a word of encouragement to you? *Good things are growing in your waiting.*

God is using these moments of unseen, unspectacular, underground growth to build you up and establish you on him—to stand you firm for the next phase he has planned for your life.

These moments aren't wasted; they're transformational. Essential, even. We can thank God knowing that he is too good to grow us without roots.

Cultivate

Wherever you find yourself waiting today—stuck in traffic during a car ride to work, left on hold while making a phone call to schedule an appointment, even in an actual waiting room—spend some time thanking God for the ways in which he's faithful to grow you during this process.

Beginning to Bud

TRUSTING IN GOD THE GARDENER

18

All for Jesus

"And whatever you do, in word or deed, do everything in the name of the Lord Jesus, giving thanks to God the Father through him."

COLOSSIANS 3:17

My arms and back were aching. My legs were covered in tiny scratches, and if I'd had a mirror handy, I'm pretty sure my hair would have looked like I'd just stepped out of a windstorm.

I was in the middle of a raspberry-picking session and it had all become a bit overwhelming. I'd been dreaming of having our own raspberry patch for a long time. It was the one thing I'd missed when we left our previous home. Now after all these years, it had finally taken off—and so had the time to care for it.

I loved it, yes. I enjoyed the serene stillness of being outdoors and the sweet goodness of freshly-picked berries, but I couldn't deny that the effort was also coming with its downsides—the scratched appendages and lengthy harvest time, to name a few.

Sometimes life works exactly like this—we spend so much time dreaming about the future, yet the very things we longed for can often come with their own laundry list of unexpected accompaniments. Maybe the spouse who you once thought was able to do no wrong has revealed a surprising list of quirks and idiosyncrasies. The home that seemed like such a blessing when you first bought it has exposed an endless demand for upkeep. The job you'd been dreaming about has come with its own share of issues—challenging coworkers or inflexible deadlines.

This is exactly why gratitude is so critical. Because, in our broken world, every good gift is also going to come with some slightly less desirable parts. And before we know it, the very things we were once so grateful for can begin to feel more like burdens than blessings.

A few years back, a friend shared with me that whenever she is doing laundry for her family, she picks up the pieces of clothing one by one, and thanks God for the owner of each item. This practical tip stayed with me as a simple way to keep a sense of gratitude in the middle of a chore that can otherwise seem so monotonous.

What if we viewed all areas of life with the same kind of attitude? What if we practiced gratitude as our knee-jerk reaction in the midst of running errands and scheduling doctor's appointments and driving from here to there?

Colossians 3:17 reminds us, "And whatever you do, in word or deed, do everything in the name of the Lord Jesus, giving thanks to God the Father through him." This means that whatever God has called us to right now—a sink full of dishes or caring for an aging parent or punching in for another workday—it's seen by the Lord. And because of this, we can give God thanks, trusting that no matter how small or insignificant our everyday may seem, all of it matters.

But here's the key: we do it *all in the name of the Lord.* That means that cleaning up after our family is no longer a chore meant solely for them—although it most certainly is a labor of love—but rather a work being offered up to God. A day at the office isn't just a chance to garner another paycheck—it's an opportunity to worship Jesus right where he has placed us. Running errands or returning phone calls or making dinner are more than simply tasks to check off our to-do list—they're gifts that glorify God when they're done in his name.

Friend, whatever God has called you to do today, I pray that you would see that no part of your life is small or insignificant to him. Offer up each day to him and watch him grow your heart in gratefulness as you do all things in the name of Jesus.

Cultivate

What is something you're responsible for every day or weekly that often ends up feeling like a chore? How can you incorporate thanksgiving into the task and see this as an opportunity to serve, worship, and be in communion with your Savior?

19

The Invitation to Peace

"And let the peace of God rule in your hearts, to which indeed you were called in one body. And be thankful."

COLOSSIANS 3:15

I received some heavy news about one of my kids a couple of weeks ago and honestly, it's been a struggle most days to keep my peace. My mind can't help wandering through details and wondering what's going to happen and worrying about what, if anything else, I should be doing. Living at peace in a world that feels anything but peaceful can be challenging, can't it?

In the Old Testament, King Jehoshaphat found himself in just this kind of place after receiving news that enemy armies from the neighboring countries of Moab and Ammon were advancing upon his kingdom. In these reports, the numbers of the armies were so large that they were described as "a great multitude" (2 Chronicles 20:2). In desperation, Jehoshaphat gathers together the people to pray. And as he does so, he closes with a powerful statement found in verse 12: "We do not know what to do, but our eyes are on you."

Anyone else ever been confronted by something that doesn't just want to steal your peace, it also wants to rob you of any hope or ability to know what to do?

I'm so thankful for the assurance found in John 14:27 that reminds us where real peace comes from. Jesus tells us, "Peace I leave with you; my peace I give to you. Not as the world gives do I give to you. Let not your hearts be troubled, neither let them be afraid."

Friend, our hearts don't need to tremble, much less be troubled, by the storms that will inevitably pass through our lives. God doesn't give us a flimsy peace or a shakable hope—through Christ we have access to peace and hope and thankfulness that isn't of this world, it's of him. How then do we access this kind of rock-solid peace over our own lives? We act out of the *truth* of it, before we sense the *feeling* of it.

This is exactly what Jehoshaphat does. As the Israelites prepare for battle, he commands those appointed as worshipers and singers to go out *before* the army. I mean, what kind of battle plan is this? But as they do, these are the words they sing: "Give thanks to the Lord, for his steadfast love endures forever" (2 Chronicles 20:21).

I don't know if this moves you as much as it does me, but they are actually giving God thanks before the victory! In order to reach their breakthrough, the people first needed to give God praise.

I believe this can teach us a powerful truth for our own lives: giving thanks is key to accessing God's peace in our lives, no matter what turmoil we face.

Gratitude isn't limited to "good days" when the sun is shining and everything seems to make sense. I believe it can be even more important to give thanks on those days when we're heading into battle against the enemy! And as we offer our praise, God's supernatural presence will overwhelm our hearts and remind us that we don't have the kind of peace the world gives—we have already overcome everything in this world through the power of Christ.

The reality is, I don't know how this situation with my child will pan out. And I'm guessing there are similar unknowns in your own life. But we can praise God and give him thanks now, knowing that he has defeated the greatest enemy and triumphed over death. We've been given a peace about our ultimate future that isn't bound by our circumstances or tied to what even makes sense. We can have peace right in the midst of the battle, knowing that God is the one who goes before us.

Let's remember, in the words of King Jehoshaphat, "Do not be afraid and do not be dismayed ... for the battle is not yours but God's" (2 Chronicles 20:15).

Cultivate

What situation in your life is feeling like a battle? I challenge you today to step forward in praise and accept the supernatural peace that is yours through faith in Christ. Turn on the worship music, maybe even sing aloud, and take some time thanking God in advance of the outcome.

20

Our Great God

*"But ask the beasts, and they will teach you; the birds of
the heavens, and they will tell you; or the bushes of the
earth, and they will teach you; and the fish of the sea
will declare to you. Who among all these does not know
that the hand of the LORD has done this?"*

JOB 12:7-9

A group of squirrelly, incoming second-graders all sat
facing one another in a very lopsided circle. I was going
around the room asking students to share a "God sighting"
from their day. It was an opportunity to get the kids to
interact while also reminding them to actively look for God's
presence in their everyday lives. I pointed toward the next
wildly waving hand—its owner a little boy half-standing
with excitement at the prospect of sharing his finding. "The
clouds!" he beamed.

"Yes," I encouraged as I made my way on to the next
volunteer. "Trees!" another shouted out. "My friends!" "The
flowers!" A shy voice piped up at my side. "Teacher, I see God
when I'm swimming."

Maybe these responses seem a bit childish, but as I was listening, I noticed how many students listed creation as the place where they could see God. The Scriptures themselves point to this truth, telling us in Romans 1:20, "For his invisible attributes, namely, his eternal power and divine nature, have been clearly perceived, ever since the creation of the world, in the things that have been made. So [people] are without excuse."

This means that we can see the character of God—his awesomeness and his power and even his eternal goodness— through the good world that he's created. In fact, it says in Romans that we are without excuse because creation itself testifies about its Creator.

It sounds odd, but one of my favorite spaces to see God is in my raspberry patch. Each morning in the summer and early fall, I head out to the plot alongside our garage and make my way through the prickly canes, plucking off the ripe fruit and dropping it in my basket while I thank God for the beauty and provision of a simple berry. Watching them grow, I'm reminded that each one has been lovingly given the power to sprout and mature and become ready to eat by our God. He is present in all creation, from the tallest, most majestic mountain to the tiniest seed.

Recently I stumbled upon these words in Job 12:7-9 and I had to smile. It says, "Ask the beasts, and they will teach you; the birds of the heavens, and they will tell you; or the *bushes of the earth,* and they will teach you; and the fish of the sea will declare to you. Who among all these does not know that the hand of the LORD has done this?"

Perhaps a raspberry patch isn't such a strange place to see God, after all.

I think those second-graders understand something we grown-ups so often forget—the world is full of wonder. From the clouds in the sky, to the trees on the way to work, to the friends and family we're surrounded by every day—each one is a blessed gift from our Creator God. Every small detail is divinely designed by a heavenly Father who orchestrated it all to breathe into creation this truth: *I am here.*

In choosing the way of gratefulness, we stay in awe of normality, no matter how old we get. It's how we remain in wonder of God's greatness, even for a sight we've seen a million times before. It's how we notice God's fingerprint in the minute moments of our lives.

We refuse to succumb to the idea that familiarity must grow into ingratitude. We refuse to overlook the ordinary—really, none of it is. Every morning sunrise, every new plant budding, each breath we take, is a taste of God's goodness and grace.

Friends, this is the power of seeing God in our world. This is the beauty behind the everyday—God is here. We have a Creator who is present in every detail of our lives. May we open our eyes to the wonder and majesty all around us through giving thanks.

Cultivate

Make a commitment to get outside today, even for just a few moments, so you can pay attention to the small, delicate details of creation and thank God for being the awesome yet personal Creator that he is. If you can't fit that in your calendar for today, schedule a time coming up where you can enjoy some time outdoors in God's presence.

21

The Good Gardener

"And we know that for those who love God all things work together for good, for those who are called according to his purpose."

ROMANS 8:28

I had just read the words of Psalm 33:20-22 when I felt tears pricking the corners of my eyes: "We put our hope in the Lord; he is our protector and our help. We are glad because of him; we trust in his holy name. May your constant love be with us, Lord, as we put our hope in you" (GNT). In my journal, I scribbled the words, "Lord, thank you for breaking apart everything that I stood on apart from you."

Those are hard words, aren't they? As I've found myself confronted by heartache and tragedy over these past several years, I've cried more tears than I can count, questioned more than I'd like to admit, and wondered whether any of these circumstances would ever truly turn out good.

But I've also begun to realize that *nothing else has brought me closer to Christ.*

The things that have been stripped away from my world were like unsteady legs that I'd been trying to build my life upon. And through the pain of them being pulled out from under me, I've learned that nothing else can provide a solid footing for my life apart from Christ. Ever so slowly, I'm beginning to feel thankful for it.

That sounds strange, doesn't it? But now I see that God was realigning my heart. He was teaching me firsthand how the only safe place for hope is in *him*. Even in the midst of my most awful, heart-wrenching moments, God was using it all for good.

That's the message of Romans 8:28: "We know that in all things God works for good with those who love him, those whom he has called according to his purpose" (GNT). It's a passage I've known and loved since I was a child. In fact, I requested it to be read at our wedding. But I think sometimes it's easy for us to overlook two key words: *all things.*

Yes, God does work everything together for good, but perhaps the even greater message is that our Father uses *all things*—the messy, hard, and even terrible things—to work together to create his best for our lives. *Nothing is so bad that God can't work good through it.*

This is the faithful gardener who is tending the soil of our hearts to grow something beautiful. He alone knows what's best for us. John 15:1-2 reminds us, "I am the true vine, and my Father is the vinedresser. Every branch in me that does not bear fruit he takes away, and every branch that does bear fruit he prunes, that it may bear more fruit." We can trust that our God is always growing us—even when it feels as though something precious has been pruned off—so that our lives can bear much fruit.

When we trust in the Lord through thanksgiving, we come to see the soil of our suffering not as worthless but as the ground where he is working for our good.

We recognize that anything that brings us closer to Christ is a blessing. Jesus goes on to say in John 15:9, "As the Father has loved me, so have I loved you. Abide in my love." This love is the certainty that we can grasp hold of when we are faced with pain. The one who is tending to our lives, carefully pruning and shaping, is the same Father who did not spare his own Son to save us. Out of the worst possible suffering came the most beautiful expression of his loving nature. The surest way we can stay grounded in this truth is to abide in that love through giving him thanks.

Even when it seems impossible to see, our deepest hurts and hardships aren't being wasted—they're in the hands of the good gardener who is working everything together to bring about his best for our lives.

Will you pray with me?

Lord, I confess that sometimes it's difficult to see the good that you're working out of my life. As I walk through these spaces of unforeseen goodness, will you help me to trust you more? Lord, through the power of your Holy Spirit, I choose to believe that you are a good God who is always working all things for good. I give you thanks that regardless of what I'm going through, you never change and your love never fails. In Jesus' name, Amen.

22

Freedom

"The thief comes only to steal and kill and destroy. I came that they may have life and have it abundantly."

JOHN 10:10

I still remember the day I fully surrendered my life to Christ. Sure, I had grown up in the church and heard Bible stories umpteen times and even been baptized years before as a child, but something happened one sunny day as I stood staring out of the window and talked to God. As I gazed up at the white, puffy clouds parading their way across a brilliant blue sky, I whispered, "I trust you alone to save me."

Nothing has impacted my life more. And if you are a believer, too, I wholeheartedly believe there is no greater gift that God has given you than this—the salvation you've gained through Jesus Christ your Savior.

Now if you're a person who's grown up in church and heard this since you were a child, I know how familiar it may all sound. But I pray that we would never start taking this truth as common—*God's greatest gift to us is Jesus Christ.*

Romans 5:8 tells us, "But God demonstrates his own love for us in this; while we were still sinners, Christ died for us" (NIV). The way God showed his love toward us was by giving us, in our helplessness and sin, the most amazing gift; he made the payment for all our wrongdoing that has now granted us eternal life through Jesus Christ. How long has it been since you rejoiced or simply thanked God for that gift of salvation?

And yet, Christ didn't only die and rise again so that we would know our eternal destination was secure—he died so that we could live in freedom in our daily lives. If you've accepted Jesus as your Savior, you've not only been granted the freedom of knowing you'll spend eternity with Jesus but you've been gifted the opportunity to experience this freedom in your life here and now.

It means that when you're on the way to work and battling worry and anxiety about the future, you have the freedom to live in the truth that God is for you and is working all things together for your good (Romans 8:28). It means that when you find yourself losing patience with your kids—*yet again*—you have the freedom to accept his mercies that are brand new for you every day (Lamentations 3:22). It means that when you are feeling burdened by regret and guilt over the past, you can live in the knowledge that you've been set free from every weight of sin and shame (Romans 6:22).

Jesus himself explains it like this: "The thief comes only to steal and kill and destroy. I came that they may have life and have it abundantly" (John 10:10). Jesus has given us the freedom to live life to the fullest—life that has an eternal significance and a heavenly perspective no matter what we may be facing. We are free, in every sense of the word.

This testimony of what God has done in our lives and how he has brought us from death to life is one of the greatest weapons we have against the tactics of the enemy. Revelation

12:11 tells us, "And they have conquered [Satan] by the blood of the Lamb and by the word of their testimony." We can live in real, everyday abundance by recalling with thankfulness the freedom we've been given through the power of his sacrifice and the testimony of its impact on our own lives.

Friend, have you ever stopped to consider the power of your testimony? Are you living in the true, abundant freedom that Christ purchased for you on the cross? Jesus came to earth not just to set you free after death—he came to make you free in every aspect of your life. Free from the grave, free from the lies of the enemy, and from every other thing that would try to separate you from the love of Christ. What a gift.

Cultivate

Have you ever taken the time to write down your testimony or share this powerful witness with another? Or if you haven't yet made the decision to follow Christ, what are the things holding you back from finding this freedom in your own life? As we spend some time today reflecting on the gift of salvation, let's thank him for the freedom he offers us through his sacrifice, both for eternity and for every day of our earthly lives.

Bringing in the Harvest

**RECEIVING THE BLESSINGS
GOD GIVES TO EVERY BELIEVER**

23

Joy Really is Jesus

"Do not be grieved, for the joy of the LORD is your strength."

NEHEMIAH 8:10

"Ibelieve God is bringing you into a season of joy."

When I heard these words—spoken by a dear friend of mine who'd taken me under her wing in the past few years—I paused. We were seated across from one another at a local coffee shop, the sounds of cups clinking and conversations flowing all around, and I had just finished spilling out the latest drama in a seemingly never-ending season of suffering.

Joy? What on earth did I know about joy?

But her words gave me pause. And a deep sense of consideration. Was I living in the joy of the Lord? And if not, then why not? Nehemiah 8:10 reminds us, "Do not be grieved, for the joy of the LORD is your strength."

What does it mean to have this joy of the Lord? It's simply this—the joy of having Jesus.

This is Jesus who came as a Servant-King, was born into poverty, grew up as a humble carpenter, and experienced all the pain, sorrow, and frustration of life. This is Jesus who stopped and took time to heal and speak with thousands of desperate people wherever he walked. This is Jesus who cooked breakfast for his followers (John 21:9); washed their feet (John 13:4-12); and ultimately subjected himself to the pain and suffering of the cross and the grave; who stepped out of the tomb after three days, defeating death once and for all so that you and I don't have to live in guilt and fear. The joy we have is to know this same Jesus personally and intimately—always with us by his Spirit and speaking to us through his word.

"Looking to Jesus" is what sustains our joy and helps us endure, no matter our circumstances, as Hebrews 12:2 tells us. This is what Jesus himself exemplified: "The founder and perfecter of our faith, who for the joy that was set before him endured the cross, despising the shame, and is seated at the right hand of the throne of God." Like Jesus, we can look at every aspect of our lives—even the crosses we have to bear—as a means to joy, thanking God that he can use the hardest parts of our story for his glory.

Friend, God wants so much more for us than just plodding our way through the next thing. He has better things planned for us than simply surviving our hard times or settling for temporary, sporadic joy. In Psalm 16, David says: "I say to the LORD, 'You are my Lord; I have no good apart from you'" (v 2). Even in desperation, when all else seems lost, David declares that the Lord is "my chosen portion and my cup" (v 5) and that "the lines have fallen for me in pleasant places; indeed, I have a beautiful inheritance" (v 6). How much more can we claim this, having seen the fulfillment of God's promise of a Savior, having heard the wonderful words of Jesus, and having known the beauty of his character.

David says, "I have set the LORD always before me ... Therefore my heart is glad, and my whole being rejoices" (v 8-9). As believers in Christ, we have the good, kind, powerful, forgiving presence of Jesus in our very being at all times! Are you ready to make the joy of the Lord your strength? Are you ready to live in the joy-filled confidence of trusting him?

Give thanks for everything Jesus is and you will deepen your relationship with him day by day; your thanksgiving will grow into joy. This alone is your strength: the joy of truly knowing his love and trusting him with your life.

Will you pray with me?

Dear Jesus, today I want to thank you for the gift of you. Thank you for reminding me that no matter what changes in my life or what I go through, I will always have you. Lord, I admit that there are times in life when the idea of being joyful feels impossible. And yet I'm discovering that right in these very moments is where you offer the joy of yourself. Lord, I pray that this alone would be my strength—the joy of having you. In your name, Amen.

24

All Things Beautiful

"He has made everything beautiful in its time. Also, he has put eternity into man's heart, yet so that he cannot find out what God has done from the beginning to the end."

ECCLESIASTES 3:11

"Well God, I can't wait to see what good you're going to work out of *this.*"

I happened to be walking on the treadmill when this silent prayer rolled through my brain. I had just received the news about yet another seeming setback, and frankly, I was taken aback at my own response. For years, my initial reaction would have been to worry or fret when issues like this popped up, but recently God had been growing something in my life—the confidence and trust of seeing from the other side.

This is what Scripture is talking about when it tells us in Ecclesiastes 3:11, "He has made everything beautiful in its time. Also, he has put eternity into man's heart, yet so that he cannot find out what God has done from the beginning to the end."

As believers, we get to live in grateful expectancy and confident anticipation of this promised beauty. Through giving thanks, God is inviting us into the peace-filled life of trusting that he really is working everything together in our lives to build something beautiful. This means that whether we're faced with job loss or relationship struggles or the inconveniences and challenges of everyday life, we choose to live in the confident expectancy of this beauty—even if it's a beauty that's yet to be seen.

I've often found myself stuck in this space of trying to figure out what God is doing "from the beginning to the end." I've struggled to make sense out of the nonsensical or find purpose in the painful, all the while believing that the beauty is something that I should be able to see *right now.*

Just this past week, my four-year-old daughter came home from Sunday school with a plastic bag filled with carrot seeds and wet cotton balls. The moment we got inside the house she insisted they needed water—yet again—so they would start growing. In her mind, those itty-bitty seeds surely should have sprung up on the ride home from church!

As silly as it is to expect physical seeds to begin sprouting immediately, why do I expect the spiritual seeds in my life to be any different? There's one phrase of that Ecclesiastes verse that's critical to remember: *in its time.*

We praise God ahead of time, in full confidence that fruitfulness will bloom in our lives after the long stretch of hidden roots deepening in the dark. We can thank God in advance of the harvest, trusting and believing that he truly is growing something beautiful in the garden of our hearts.

And friend, can I tell you that you get to live in the joy of that. You get to walk in the peace of that promise. You can grab hold of this day-in, day-out hope that God *is* growing something beautiful in your life, even if it's a harvest you have yet to see.

We don't have to piece together our broken pieces and try to make them beautiful ourselves. We don't even have to understand what God is doing. But we can give him thanks that he is using it all—even the ugliest parts of our story—to paint a beautiful picture that ultimately points us all toward the hope of *him*.

Thanks be to God that we get to live with this confident assurance—God is using it all to bring in a bountiful harvest in our hearts, and it's going to be beautiful.

Cultivate
Can you think of something in your life that is now bearing fruit or a source of beauty that was once buried under confusion or darkness? Spend time praising God for that timing. Now think of a current situation that you don't understand—can you thank God ahead of time for the way he will bring beauty from ashes, if only in eternity?

25

God's Words

"Everyone then who hears these words of mine and does them will be like a wise man who built his house on the rock. And the rain fell, and the floods came, and the winds blew and beat on that house, but it did not fall, because it had been founded on the rock."

MATTHEW 7:24-25

These are the elements of my morning routine—my favorite throw blanket draped across my lap, my Bible and a notebook spread open, and a steamy mug of tea by my side.

For years I longed for this, or perhaps a better description would be, *I beat myself up about this.* I'd welcome a new year by diving into a Bible plan with all the excitement and expectation of a fresh start, only to find myself fizzling out a few weeks later after falling behind a day or two.

But then, several years ago, something changed—I whole-heartedly, deep-down-in-my-soul accepted grace. I finally believed and fully received that God's grace was enough for me, whether or not I read my Bible every day or grew impatient with my kids or fell short in a million other ways. And I can't think of anything else that has transformed—or steadied—my life like founding it on the word of God.

Jesus makes a similar comparison in Matthew 7, where he uses the metaphor of building a house to show the importance of planting our lives on this truth. "Everyone then who hears these words of mine and does them will be like a wise man who built his house on the rock. And the rain fell, and the floods came, and the winds blew and beat on that house, but it did not fall, because it had been founded on the rock" (Matthew 7:24-25).

Oh, can I tell you that the floods have come and the rain has fallen and the winds have sure tried to blow their way through my life! But you know what else I can tell you? *My house hasn't fallen.*

And friend, I believe this is the power of building our lives on the word of God. Whatever storms may come our way, whatever trials we may face, our lives will never be shaken when we're planted on Jesus and obeying his word.

Hebrews 4:12 describes this word as "living and active"; it is a guide that applies in every situation and discerns "the thoughts and intentions of the heart." When the world feels dark and confusing, it is a "lamp to my feet and a light to my path" (Psalm 119:105). God's word is essential for teaching and training in righteousness (2 Timothy 3:16-17), endures forever (1 Peter 1:25), is continually at work within us (1 Thessalonians 2:13), and promises to never return back void (Isaiah 55:11). God's word is so essential that Matthew 4:4 actually refers to it as the bread of life.

Scripture is the solid ground that God has given us to make us "wise" and to provide us with safety through the storms. When we put God's words into practice, when we meditate on them and pray through them and store them up in our heart, we accept his word as more than just a guidebook.

We will know it to be the most essential thing we need as a believer—the very sustenance of life. It's not just that it's profitable for our growth; the word is how we get to know God himself. Isn't that remarkable?

Living in a place where copies of the Bible are plentiful is such a gift. We have constant and direct access to God's voice through the power of his word. Everything else about our world can shift in an instant—our health, our finances, our job situations, our own families—but the truth of God's word won't ever shift or change. As it says in Matthew 24:35, "Heaven and earth will pass away, but my words will not pass away."

This is what we can build our lives on, the rock we can stand firm on that won't ever give way. This is the gift that God has given to every believer—his personal love letter that leads and uplifts and is forever unshakable no matter what storms may come our way.

Oh, thank God for the firm foundation of his word.

Cultivate

Praise God for this gift! Use Psalm 119 as a starting point to thank God for the wonder of his word.

If you want to get to know God better through his word, begin by choosing one verse (or more, if you like!) that you want to commit to memory. Read it out loud five times, write it out by hand, tape it to a bathroom mirror or listen to it read aloud on a Bible app.

26

The Blessing of the Body

"And above all these put on love, which binds everything together in perfect harmony. And let the peace of Christ rule in your hearts, to which indeed you were called in one body. And be thankful."

COLOSSIANS 3:14-15

Recently, I had the sheer joy of getting to lead worship for another local church's baptism service. Some dear friends of ours serve as pastors there, and since our family was planning to come and celebrate their daughter's baptism with them, they had asked if I would also be willing to lead the music. I eagerly accepted.

That morning, as I watched from my spot behind the piano, I was overcome with tears as I listened to story after story of God's redemption. A rough, tattoo-covered man shared how God had rescued him from substance abuse and gang violence. A mother and son told their story of starting to watch the services online and finding hope and healing through the preaching of the gospel. Our friends' precious daughter shared her simple, heartfelt desire to love Jesus and serve him. The stories went on and on, with nearly a dozen baptized in this church of less than 100.

After the service we joined together for a potluck meal where plates were piled high with homemade casseroles and cold-cut sandwiches and colorful salads. Children scurried around the dessert selection, and groups chatted around large tables while church ladies busied themselves in the kitchen. I looked around at this loving family of God coming together in community and wondered if sometimes we've become so inundated with stories of the scandals and failings within the church that too often we miss this—the tremendous blessing that God has given to us in the body of Christ, his church.

This body of believers is God's gift to us—it equips us with a foundation of doctrine and instruction (Romans 15:14), encouragement and support (Acts 2:42), prayerful concern (Philippians 4:6-7), and practical care (James 1:27). Ultimately, it is the place where the Great Commission can be fulfilled (Matthew 28:18-20).

That's why these words from Colossians 3:14-15 are such an important reminder as we consider our own place within the body. It says, "And above all these put on love, which binds everything together in perfect harmony. And let the peace of Christ rule in your hearts, to which indeed you were called in one body. And be thankful."

Did you catch that? The two ingredients necessary for discovering peace and harmony within the church are, firstly, love and, lastly, thankfulness. These two things are what we as believers are called to actively employ—to "put on love" and "be thankful"—both contribute to "perfect harmony" and "the peace of Christ."

Yes, there certainly will be times and circumstances where the challenges within the church seem more obvious than the blessings, but we can still actively choose to clothe ourselves in love and gratitude for this wonderful gift God has given us.

Jesus thought this was so important that it was the sole descriptor he used when he wanted to describe his followers, telling us in John 13:35, "By this all people will know that you are my disciples, if you have love for one another."

Let's thank God today for the many brothers and sisters he's given us in the body of Christ. What a gift it is to be part of an international as well as local family, in which we can edify one another, worship together, and share in the good news of the gospel. Then we can watch as God turns that thankfulness to greater love. This is the example we've been given in Jesus and his incredible love for his bride, the church; as it says in Ephesians 5:25, "Christ loved the church and gave himself up for her."

Do you consider this body that you're a part of as a gift? God certainly does.

Cultivate

Today praise God for your local church family or the church as a whole. Are there any ways in which you could connect with your church more deeply—perhaps joining a small group or sending a thank-you letter to one of your leaders? Simply thank God for the gift and blessing he has given you through his bride.

27

The Truth about Fruitfulness

"Let your light shine before others, so that they may see your
good works and give glory to your Father who is in heaven."

MATTHEW 5:16

I remember walking outside, that first year we grew pumpkins, only to be dismayed to see that the vines had begun to shrivel up. Inwardly I began reprimanding myself, wondering why I had not remembered to water them more or how I could have forgotten to pay better attention to their growth.

Except, upon closer inspection, I noticed something else. The pumpkins themselves were just fine. In fact, they had begun to lose the bright green signs of youthfulness and had started to take on their familiar orangish hue.

After some further reading, my observations were confirmed—this was exactly what the plants required in order to fully mature. This letting go—this drying up that at first glance seemed like dying—was in fact the process necessary for the pumpkin to be ready to harvest.

As I made my way through the garden I began to ponder a strange question—what does the plant get for all of this hard work? Is there any benefit for all its fruitfulness?

And the conclusion I came to was: *fruitfulness isn't for the plant—it's for others.*

Plants themselves don't stand to gain anything by growing good fruit. Their fruitfulness goes on to benefit those who eat the fruit or the new plants that follow. The plant has fulfilled its purpose. But the impact of its fruit goes on.

Once again, I'm struck by how these patterns in nature are reflected in our spiritual lives.

As we grow and begin to reap the harvest of gratitude in our lives, our purpose is not to turn into nicer people or lead more carefree lives—though I do believe both may be side-effects of living more gratefully. Our fruitfulness isn't primarily for us. We bear fruit so that the richness and nourishment of God's goodness blooms out of our lives and into a world that so desperately needs to see him—at our workplace, in our homes, wherever we may go.

This transformation first begins at salvation. Romans 8:29 says, "For those whom he foreknew he also predestined to be conformed to the image of his Son, in order that he might be the firstborn among many brothers." This is God's greatest desire for each of our lives—that we would be made to look more like his Son.

Just as Jesus shines his light into the world through his obedience and submission to his Father, so our commitment to giving thanks points others to the goodness and faithfulness of our God. Matthew 5:16 tells us, "Let your light shine before others, so that they may see your good works and give glory to your Father who is in heaven."

The light that shines through our lives when we draw close to God serves as a beacon to point others straight to the risen Savior. This is our mission as we live life on this side of eternity—to let *his* light radiate through us and out into the world.

And the ultimate outcome of it all? God is glorified.

As we've journeyed together over these past chapters, that's my prayer for both of us. That as our hearts are transformed and we are conformed more to the image of Christ, God would get all the glory.

Is that the desire of your heart? Is that the kind of life you want to lead—a life overflowing with gratefulness that is a blessing to your family and your church and everyone around you? Keep giving him thanks. Allow the Holy Spirit to transform your heart into a shining replication of Jesus that beams his light for all to see. May the beautiful fruit of gratefulness continue to be harvested from your life so that, ultimately, God receives the glory.

Will you pray with me?

God, thank you for the ways you're transforming my heart so that I look more like your Son. As I begin harvesting some of the blessings of gratefulness, I praise you for the privilege it is to be a beacon of your light to bless my family, friends, church, and everyone else I come into contact with. Thank you for using every little thing so that you may be glorified in me. In Jesus' name, Amen.

28

The Comforter

"But the fruit of the Spirit is love, joy, peace, patience, kindness, goodness, faithfulness, gentleness, self-control; against such things there is no law."

GALATIANS 5:22-23

I'll never forget the afternoon I felt God asking me to share a word of encouragement with my neighbor. While on a walk, pulling my son behind me in a wagon, my eyes landed on a woman seated on her front porch. Out of nowhere, I felt God speak to my heart—*Go tell her I love her.*

Now if you're anything like me, the last thing you want to do is approach someone you've never met and give them a message, having no idea how it might be received. So I headed straight past, pretending I hadn't heard a thing.

Except on the way back home I felt that same nudge. I wish I could tell you I obeyed... but I walked past *again.* As I returned to the house, arguing inwardly, I made this little promise—if she was still there when I looked out of my window, I'd speak to her.

Lo and behold, there she was.

So back out I headed, heart beating furiously and with all the reasons why this lady would think I was crazy rolling around my head. As I introduced myself and delivered this message, imagine my shock when this neighbor not only embraced me but began crying as she heard these words. She wasn't just willing to listen, she'd been in the middle of praying for just this kind of confirmation.

Only God.

I know this experience isn't typical, but I do believe that God wants to actively speak and guide us through our lives. In John 16:7, Jesus makes a pretty radical statement, telling his followers, "It is to your advantage that I go away, for if I do not go away, the Helper will not come to you. But if I go, I will send him to you."

Doesn't the idea of walking with Jesus face to face sound like the ultimate spiritual experience? And yet Jesus says he's given us something *even better*—the gift of the Holy Spirit.

Ephesians 1:14 calls this the "guarantee of our inheritance." At the initial moment that we're saved, God deposits a little bit of eternity into our hearts, and we receive the divine down-payment that heaven is our forever home.

But the Holy Spirit is so much more than an insurance policy. Jesus goes on to tell us in verse 13, "When the Spirit of truth comes, he will guide you into all the truth, for he will not speak on his own authority, but whatever he hears he will speak, and he will declare to you the things that are to come" (John 16:13). Just like my experience with my neighbor, God wants to guide our steps as he prepares us for the things "that are to come."

In addition, Scripture tells us that the Holy Spirit is our helper (John 14:26) who assists us in prayer (Jude 1:20), renews us (Titus 3:5), brings us comfort (1 Thessalonians 1:6), and causes us to overflow with hope (Romans 15:13). The whole process of maturing as a Christian is an act of God within us as we surrender to the work he wants to do through the power of his Spirit.

As the Holy Spirit abides and dwells in the soil of our hearts, our lives will ultimately burst forth with this growing evidence of his presence. This is what Galatians 5:22-23 refers to as "the fruit of the Spirit [being] love, joy, peace, patience, kindness, goodness, faithfulness, gentleness, self-control."

Don't you want to reap the rewards of more joy and peace in your own life? Wouldn't you love to live a life filled with more faithfulness, gentleness, and self-control? Then thank the Lord that you've already been given everything you need! 2 Peter 1:3 reminds us, "His divine power has granted to us all things that pertain to life and godliness, through the knowledge of him who called us to his own glory and excellence."

What a blessing to know that God has already given us everything we need *in him*. The answer to living a more grateful life isn't about us trying more but *relying more*.

We really do have something even better than Jesus' physical presence on earth—we have his Spirit inside us. He is guiding us, transforming us, and growing the godly fruit inside our hearts that day by day makes us look more like Jesus. What a blessed assurance of the hope that is ours.

Cultivate

Today as you are confronted with moments where you are tempted to feel impatient or lose your peace or struggle with other fruits of the Spirit, I want to challenge you not to see these as failures but as opportunities for God to grow you. Ask the Holy Spirit to fill you and guide you and then give thanks for the work he's already done in you.

29

Eternity

"What no eye has seen, nor ear heard, nor the heart of man imagined, what God has prepared for those who love him."

1 CORINTHIANS 2:9

How would my life change if I truly lived like heaven was real?

I think this is an important question to ask ourselves—and to evaluate our lives with—because heaven *is* real! And yet how often I fail to act accordingly.

Ephesians 6:17 refers to the "helmet of salvation" as part of the armor of God that we need to stand firm. I don't think a single one of us would enter into a war zone without a helmet protecting our heads, but how often do we go through the battles of life without this protective hope of salvation over our minds? This confidence that we are saved and heaven is our forever home is what shields our thinking from whatever fiery darts the enemy tries to throw our way.

I wonder whether a lot of the things that disappoint us or get us down here on earth would be drowned out if we only remembered where we are headed. 1 Corinthians 2:9 reminds us, "But as it is written, 'What no eye has seen, nor ear heard, nor the heart of man imagined, what God has prepared for those who love him'" (1 Corinthians 2:9).

Friend, God has indeed created a place for us which is so far beyond our wildest dreams, we can't even begin to imagine it! And yet we are called to live with this place in full view. This is the kind of eternal perspective that God is inviting us to live in accordance with, as believers in Christ.

Revelation 21:1-4 paints the picture of what we have to look forward to: "Then I saw a new heaven and a new earth, for the first heaven and the first earth had passed away, and the sea was no more. And I saw the holy city, new Jerusalem, coming down out of heaven from God, prepared as a bride adorned for her husband. And I heard a loud voice from the throne saying, "Behold, the dwelling place of God is with man. He will dwell with them, and they will be his people, and God himself will be with them as their God. He will wipe away every tear from their eyes, and death shall be no more, neither shall there be mourning, nor crying, nor pain anymore, for the former things have passed away."

Gone will be the days of tears over broken relationships, grieving over goodbyes that seem too soon, or the aches and pains of an aging body. Instead, we will live in an unbroken eternity of perfect peace and harmony.

But above all that, *God himself* will be with us. No longer will we view things "through a glass, darkly" (1 Corinthians 13:12); here we will stand before God, finally understanding the things we simply couldn't make out clearly on this side of eternity.

We can't begin to imagine the beauty and majesty of heaven, but keeping in mind that we're heading to be with Jesus will give us a thankful outlook despite our struggles. This is the type of eternal perspective that 2 Corinthians

4:17-18 encourages us to take on when it says, "We view our slight, short-lived troubles in the light of eternity. We see our difficulties as the substance that produces for us an eternal, weighty glory far beyond all comparison, because we don't focus our attention on what is seen but on what is unseen" (TPT).

How do we live like heaven is real? We can see our lives through the light of eternity by continually giving God thanks for our salvation and eternal home.

We get to live in the knowledge that, in the end, everything works out right. And thanks be to God, it's going to be so far beyond anything we can fathom. A sparkling city; the family of God in harmony together; the beauty and peace of finally being together with our Lord Jesus. With the helmet of salvation firmly planted on our heads and hope in our hearts, we know that our salvation is more than secure—it's forever settled in Christ.

Cultivate

God has given us so many beautiful promises about the future home he is preparing for us. Choose one (or more!) of these passages to dwell on and thank him for the promise of eternity: John 14:1-7; Matthew 6:19-21; Revelation 21:10-27; Revelation 22: 1-5; Hebrews 11:13-16.

30

Ultimately, Hope

"We have this as a sure and steadfast anchor of the soul, a hope that enters into the inner place behind the curtain."

HEBREWS 6:19

As we close this journey of gratitude together, I pray that ultimately, what you have gathered is *hope*. No matter what you're going through, no matter how your life currently looks, you can give thanks for the hope you have in Jesus.

We don't live untethered in this world. We don't need to be tossed and turned about by the storms that come our way. We have been given a solid anchor for our lives through the sure hope of Jesus Christ.

Hebrews 6:19 tells us, "We have this as a sure and steadfast anchor of the soul, a hope that enters into the inner place behind the curtain." Friend, we have a hope that goes beyond our present circumstances and past failings and actually "enters into the inner place behind the curtain." Do you realize what this means? This hope brings us into the inner presence of God.

During Old Testament times, when the presence of God dwelt in the temple, the only person qualified to enter this most holy place was the Levitical priest—and this was only once a year during the Day of Atonement. The entire event was an intricate process which required the priest to wear specific garments and perform ceremonial washing prior to entering into the tabernacle. This was followed by the sacrificial offering of a goat and bull whose blood was then brought into the Holy of Holies to be sprinkled on the Ark of the Covenant. After this, no one would enter the space again for another full year.

But at the time of Jesus' crucifixion, Matthew 27:51 tells us, "And behold, the curtain of the temple was torn in two, from top to bottom." This space that had once been reserved solely for the priesthood is now split wide to welcome anyone who puts their faith and trust in Christ. This means that we as believers have access to a hope that goes beyond our earthly understanding and brings us into the Holy of Holies of God's presence.

And what's even more amazing? We aren't limited to this just once a year. We are welcomed into the presence of God at any time, at any place, through the sacrifice of his Son.

As believers, we have access to unmatched hope because of the Immanuel presence of Christ and the indwelling of his Spirit. I believe God wants us to grab hold of this truth that goes beyond simply 30 days or 60 days or any other length of time.

This is my prayer: that you would be so attuned to his presence that even a morning commute or a moment washing dishes might become an opportunity to experience and delight in God's presence. I pray that you might be so filled with his Spirit that even your ordinary, everyday moments would serve as an entrance into the Holy of Holies.

We don't need more *access* into God's presence; we simply need more *awareness*.

The beautiful power of giving God thanks grows in our hearts a truth that's been here all along, pointing us to a God who is ever-constant. Gratitude carries us beyond our present circumstances, and—through the power of the cross—brings us into the very sanctuary of God's presence. No longer are we separated from God by the veil of our own sinfulness or the reality of our circumstances, but we are drawn close through the hope we have in Christ.

Will we go beyond the veil and into the inner presence of God? No longer needing to do anything to atone for our sins but instead giving a sacrifice of praise?

As we wind up this journey of gratitude, I pray that you've discovered this too: in our hard and heavy, in our mundane and ordinary, in our exciting and everyday—our God stays. And more than that, he welcomes us in as his child. Close. Right into the loving relationship of Father, Son, and Spirit.

The foundation of our gratefulness is unshakable because our hope is eternally unchangeable. And the only access we need is Jesus Christ.

Cultivate
Today and every day let's thank God for the confident assurances of hope he has given us. Choose one (or more!) of these passages to dwell on: Romans 15:13; Isaiah 40:31; 1 Peter 1:3; Hebrews 6:19.

Acknowledgments

To my amazing family, who have watched first-hand as I have stumbled my way through writing and living this book while slowly learning to live gratefully myself. Particularly to my husband, Jason, who's run dinners and shuffled kids around and kept the house together while I've pined away a Sunday afternoon at Havana. I'm grateful for you, and I hope you can see your hand all over these pages, too.

To my amazing editor, Catherine Bernard. I had this preconceived notion that working with an editor would be like having a teacher standing over my shoulder with a giant red pen ready to catch any of my mistakes, but you've been the ultimate encourager through this entire process. You've stretched me when you knew I could push deeper into God's word and challenged me to fight harder for just the right words. You've truly made me a better writer.

To my publisher, The Good Book Company, for giving a rather new, fresh-faced author a chance and offering all the support through the entire journey. To Katy Morgan, who believed in this book from the very beginning and went to bat for an idea before I could even see it myself. To the entire team who worked together to finalize the cover design and marketing and helped shape this book into what it is today.

To my church family, though unnamed, your stories and impact fill so many of these pages. I'm so grateful to get to do life with you and for the ways you've taught me what a blessed gift it is to be a part of the body of Christ.

To my parents and grandparents, who've constantly checked in and asked me how the project is going and shown me your support in a million little ways. It means the world to know that I have you on my side and, most of all, for your countless prayers. What a blessing you are.

Gratitude Journal

GROWING IN THANKFULNESS

Grateful

Allison Brost

Grateful

Allison Brost

Grateful

Grateful

Grateful

Grateful

BIBLICAL | RELEVANT | ACCESSIBLE

At The Good Book Company we are dedicated to helping Christians and local churches grow. We believe that God's growth process always starts with hearing clearly what he has said to us through his timeless and flawless word—the Bible.

Ever since we opened our doors in 1991, we have been striving to produce resources that are biblical, relevant, and accessible. By God's grace, we have grown to become an international publisher, encouraging ordinary Christians of every age and stage and every background and denomination to live for Christ day by day and equipping churches to grow in their knowledge of God, their love for one another, and the effectiveness of their outreach.

Call one of our friendly team for a discussion of your needs or visit one of our local websites for more information on the resources and services we provide.

Your friends at The Good Book Company

thegoodbook.com | thegoodbook.co.uk
thegoodbook.com.au | thegoodbook.co.nz
thegoodbook.co.in